AF506375
AF506375

Other Books in the ✿S4N Pocket Poems Series

Walt Whitman, *Song of Myself: 1855 Edition* | 978-0979870767
Walt Whitman, *Song of Myself: 1892 Edition* | 978-0979870774
Alfred Tennyson, *In Memoriam* | 978-0979870798
W. B. Yeats, *Selected Early Poems* | 978-0-9798707-8-1
Robert Frost, *A Boy's Will & North of Boston* | 979-8-9851611-0-6
William Wordsworth, *Selected Poems* | 979-8-9851611-2-0
Walt Whitman, *Selected Long Poems* | 979-8-9851611-5-1
Walt Whitman, *Selected Short Poems* | 979-8-9851611-6-8
William Shakespeare, *Sonnets* | 979-8-9851611-8-2

Forthcoming titles:
Selected Poems of Edgar Allan Poe
Selected Poems of John Keats
Edgar Lee Masters: Selections from *Spoon River Anthology*
Selected Early Poems of H. D.
T. S. Eliot, *The Waste Land & Other Poems*

SELECTED LONG POEMS
WALT WHITMAN

Selected Long Poems, by Walt Whitman
© 2022 S4N Books

Cover: Walt Whitman photographed by
G. Frank Pearsall, ca. 1869-1872.
Courtesy of Ohio Wesleyan University.

ISBN: 979-8-9851611-5-1

Library of Congress Control Number: 2022935612

✤S4N Books

email: s4nbooks@outlook.com

Walt Whitman was born in 1819 on Long Island. His early life was devoted to journalism, and throughout the 1840s he contributed fiction, essays, and more traditional poetry to many New York newspapers. The first edition of Leaves of Grass *was published at the poet's own expense in 1855, and until his death in 1892 the book went through numerous revisions and expansions. While he did receive the early support of Ralph Waldo Emerson, many in the wider literary and public world were unable to forgive his frank treatment of sexuality, and the apparent formlessness of his poems. Whitman spent much of the Civil War in Washington, D.C., frequenting the soldier hospitals and caring for the wounded and dying. After the war, he become a guru of sorts to a handful of followers who vehemently defended his work, and many writers — including Oscar Wilde, in 1882 — began to make pilgrimages to Whitman's home in his later years. When he died in Camden, New Jersey, in 1892, the* New York Times *declared "we cannot call him a great poet unless we deny poetry to be an art." It is now recognized that he redefined poetry as no American, before or since.*

Note on the text:

Between 1855 and 1892, Walt Whitman published many ever-expanding editions of and supplements to *Leaves of Grass*, revising and changing nearly every poem along the way.

The poems in this book are presented in their earliest-published and most powerful form. However, since Whitman frequently changed the titles of his poems, and since the final titles are those most familiar to readers (e.g., "Crossing Brooklyn Ferry," as opposed to its original title, "Sun-Down Poem"), the titles used here are the final ones. Where necessary, the original title is given on the first page of each poem.

Song of Myself

I celebrate myself,
And what I assume you shall assume,
For every atom belonging to me as good belongs to
    you.

I loafe and invite my soul,
I lean and loafe at my ease .... observing a spear of
    summer grass.

Houses and rooms are full of perfumes .... the shelves
    are crowded with perfumes,
I breathe the fragrance myself, and know it and like
    it,
The distillation would intoxicate me also, but I shall
    not let it.

The atmosphere is not a perfume .... it has no taste of
    the distillation .... it is odorless,
It is for my mouth forever .... I am in love with it,
I will go to the bank by the wood and become
    undisguised and naked,
I am mad for it to be in contact with me.

The smoke of my own breath,

Originally untitled

Echos, ripples, and buzzed whispers .... loveroot,
    silkthread, crotch and vine,
My respiration and inspiration .... the beating of my
    heart .... the passing of blood
and air through my lungs,
The sniff of green leaves and dry leaves, and of the
    shore and darkcolored sea-rocks, and of hay in the
    barn,
The sound of the belched words of my voice ....
    words loosed to the eddies of the wind,
A few light kisses .... a few embraces .... a reaching
    around of arms,
The play of shine and shade on the trees as the supple
    boughs wag,
The delight alone or in the rush of the streets, or
    along the fields and hillsides,
The feeling of health .... the full-noon trill .... the
    song of me rising from bed and meeting the sun.

Have you reckoned a thousand acres much? Have you
    reckoned the earth much?
Have you practiced so long to learn to read?
Have you felt so proud to get at the meaning of
    poems?

Stop this day and night with me and you shall possess
    the origin of all poems,

You shall possess the good of the earth and sun .... there are millions of suns left,
You shall no longer take things at second or third hand .... nor look through the eyes of the dead .... nor feed on the spectres in books,
You shall not look through my eyes either, nor take things from me,
You shall listen to all sides and filter them from yourself.

I have heard what the talkers were talking .... the talk of the beginning and the end,
But I do not talk of the beginning or the end.

There was never any more inception than there is now,
Nor any more youth or age than there is now;
And will never be any more perfection than there is now,
Nor any more heaven or hell than there is now.

Urge and urge and urge,
Always the procreant urge of the world.

Out of the dimness opposite equals advance ....
    Always substance and increase,

Always a knit of identity .... always distinction ....
  always a breed of life.

To elaborate is no avail .... Learned and unlearned
  feel that it is so.

Sure as the most certain sure .... plumb in the
    uprights, well entretied, braced in the beams,
Stout as a horse, affectionate, haughty, electrical,
I and this mystery here we stand.

Clear and sweet is my soul .... and clear and sweet is
  all that is not my soul.

Lack one lacks both .... and the unseen is proved by
  the seen,
Till that becomes unseen and receives proof in its
  turn.

Showing the best and dividing it from the worst, age
  vexes age,
Knowing the perfect fitness and equanimity of things,
  while they discuss I am silent, and go bathe and
  admire myself.

Welcome is every organ and attribute of me, and of
  any man hearty and clean,

Not an inch nor a particle of an inch is vile, and none
  shall be less familiar than the rest.

I am satisfied .... I see, dance, laugh, sing;
As God comes a loving bedfellow and sleeps at my
  side all night and close on the peep of the day,
And leaves for me baskets covered with white towels
  bulging the house with their plenty,
Shall I postpone my acceptation and realization and
  scream at my eyes,
That they turn from gazing after and down the road,
And forthwith cipher and show me to a cent,
Exactly the contents of one, and exactly the contents
  of two, and which is ahead?

Trippers and askers surround me,
People I meet ..... the effect upon me of my early life
  .... of the ward and city I live in .... of the nation,
The latest news .... discoveries, inventions, societies
  .... authors old and new,
My dinner, dress, associates, looks, business,
  compliments, dues,
The real or fancied indifference of some man or
  woman I love,
The sickness of one of my folks – or of myself .... or
  ill-doing .... or loss or lack of money .... or
  depressions or exaltations,

They come to me days and nights and go from me
    again,
But they are not the Me myself.

Apart from the pulling and hauling stands what I am,
Stands amused, complacent, compassionating, idle,
    unitary,
Looks down, is erect, bends an arm on an impalpable
    certain rest,
Looks with its sidecurved head curious what will
    come next,
Both in and out of the game, and watching and
    wondering at it.

Backward I see in my own days where I sweated
    through fog with linguists and contenders,
I have no mockings or arguments .... I witness and
    wait.

I believe in you my soul .... the other I am must not
    abase itself to you,
And you must not be abased to the other.

Loafe with me on the grass .... loose the stop from
    your throat,
Not words, not music or rhyme I want .... not custom
    or lecture, not even the best,

Only the lull I like, the hum of your valved voice.

I mind how we lay in June, such a transparent
    summer morning;
You settled your head athwart my hips and gently
    turned over upon me,
And parted the shirt from my bosom-bone, and
    plunged your tongue to my barestript heart,
And reached till you felt my beard, and reached till
    you held my feet.

Swiftly arose and spread around me the peace and joy
    and knowledge that pass all the art and argument of
    the earth;
And I know that the hand of God is the elderhand of
    my own,
And I know that the spirit of God is the eldest brother
    of my own,
And that all the men ever born are also my brothers
    .... and the women my sisters and lovers,
And that a kelson of the creation is love;
And limitless are leaves stiff or drooping in the fields,
And brown ants in the little wells beneath them,
And mossy scabs of the wormfence, and heaped
    stones, and elder and mullen and pokeweed.

A child said, What is the grass? fetching it to me with
    full hands;
How could I answer the child? .... I do not know what
    it is any more than he.

I guess it must be the flag of my disposition, out of
    hopeful green stuff woven.

Or I guess it is the handkerchief of the Lord,
A scented gift and remembrancer designedly
    dropped,
Bearing the owner's name someway in the corners,
    that we may see and remark, and say Whose?

Or I guess the grass is itself a child .... the produced
    babe of the vegetation.

Or I guess it is a uniform hieroglyphic,
And it means, Sprouting alike in broad zones and
    narrow zones,
Growing among black folks as among white,
Kanuck, Tuckahoe, Congressman, Cuff, I give them
    the same, I receive them the same.

And now it seems to me the beautiful uncut hair of
    graves.

Tenderly will I use you curling grass,
It may be you transpire from the breasts of young
     men,
It may be if I had known them I would have loved
     them;
It may be you are from old people and from women,
     and from offspring taken soon out of their mothers'
     laps,
And here you are the mothers' laps.

This grass is very dark to be from the white heads of
     old mothers,
Darker than the colorless beards of old men,
Dark to come from under the faint red roofs of
     mouths.

O I perceive after all so many uttering tongues!
And I perceive they do not come from the roofs of
     mouths for nothing.

I wish I could translate the hints about the dead
     young men and women,
And the hints about old men and mothers, and the
     offspring taken soon out of their laps.

What do you think has become of the young and old
     men?

And what do you think has become of the women and
    children?

They are alive and well somewhere;
The smallest sprout shows there is really no death,
And if ever there was it led forward life, and does not
    wait at the end to arrest it,
And ceased the moment life appeared.

All goes onward and outward .... and nothing
    collapses,
And to die is different from what any one supposed,
    and luckier.

Has any one supposed it lucky to be born?
I hasten to inform him or her it is just as lucky to die,
    and I know it.

I pass death with the dying, and birth with the
    new-washed babe .... and am not contained
    between my hat and boots,
And peruse manifold objects, no two alike, and every
    one good,
The earth good, and the stars good, and their adjuncts
    all good.
I am not an earth nor an adjunct of an earth,

I am the mate and companion of people, all just as
    immortal and fathomless as myself;
They do not know how immortal, but I know.

Every kind for itself and its own .... for me mine male
    and female,
For me all that have been boys and that love women,
For me the man that is proud and feels how it stings
    to be slighted,
For me the sweetheart and the old maid .... for me
    mothers and the mothers of mothers,
For me lips that have smiled, eyes that have shed
    tears,
For me children and the begetters of children.

Who need be afraid of the merge?
Undrape .... you are not guilty to me, nor stale nor
    discarded,
I see through the broadcloth and gingham whether or
    no,
And am around, tenacious, acquisitive, tireless ....
    and can never be shaken away.

The little one sleeps in its cradle,
I lift the gauze and look a long time, and silently
    brush away flies with my hand.

The youngster and the redfaced girl turn aside up the
    bushy hill,
I peeringly view them from the top.

The suicide sprawls on the bloody floor of the
    bedroom.
It is so .... I witnessed the corpse .... there the pistol
    had fallen.

The blab of the pave .... the tires of carts and sluff of
    bootsoles and talk of the promenaders,
The heavy omnibus, the driver with his interrogating
    thumb, the clank of the shod horses on the granite
    floor,
The carnival of sleighs, the clinking and shouted
    jokes and pelts of snowballs;
The hurrahs for popular favorites .... the fury of
    roused mobs,
The flap of the curtained litter – the sick man inside,
    borne to the hospital,
The meeting of enemies, the sudden oath, the blows
    and fall,
The excited crowd – the policeman with his star
    quickly working his passage to the centre of the
    crowd;
The impassive stones that receive and return so many
    echoes,

The souls moving along .... are they invisible while
    the least atom of the stones is visible?
What groans of overfed or half-starved who fall on
    the flags sunstruck or in fits,
What exclamations of women taken suddenly, who
    hurry home and give birth to babes,
What living and buried speech is always vibrating
    here .... what howls restrained by decorum,
Arrests of criminals, slights, adulterous offers made,
    acceptances, rejections with convex lips,
I mind them or the resonance of them .... I come
    again and again.

The big doors of the country-barn stand open and
    ready
The dried grass of the harvest-time loads the
    slow-drawn wagon,
The clear light plays on the brown gray and green
    intertinged,
The armfuls are packed to the sagging mow:
I am there .... I help .... I came stretched atop of the
    load,
I felt its soft jolts .... one leg reclined on the other,
I jump from the crossbeams, and seize the clover and
    timothy,
And roll head over heels, and tangle my hair full of
    wisps.

Alone far in the wilds and mountains I hunt,
Wandering amazed at my own lightness and glee,
In the late afternoon choosing a safe spot to pass the
    night,
Kindling a fire and broiling the freshkilled game,
Soundly falling asleep on the gathered leaves, my dog
    and gun by my side.
The Yankee clipper is under her three skysails …. she
    cuts the sparkle and scud,
My eyes settle the land …. I bend at her prow or
    shout joyously from the deck.

The boatmen and clamdiggers arose early and
    stopped for me,
I tucked my trowser-ends in my boots and went and
    had a good time,
You should have been with us that day round the
    chowder-kettle.

I saw the marriage of the trapper in the open air in
    the far-west …. the bride was a red girl,
Her father and his friends sat nearby crosslegged and
    dumbly smoking …. they
had moccasins to their feet and large thick blankets
    hanging from their shoulders;

On a bank lounged the trapper .... he was dressed
  mostly in skins .... his luxuriant beard and curls
  protected his neck,
One hand rested on his rifle .... the other hand held
  firmly the wrist of the red girl,
She had long eyelashes .... her head was bare .... her
  coarse straight locks descended upon her
  voluptuous limbs and reached to her feet.

The runaway slave came to my house and stopped
  outside,
I heard his motions crackling the twigs of the
  woodpile,
Through the swung half-door of the kitchen I saw
  him limpsey and weak,
And went where he sat on a log, and led him in and
  assured him,
And brought water and filled a tub for his sweated
  body and bruised feet,
And gave him a room that entered from my own, and
  gave him some coarse clean clothes,
And remember perfectly well his revolving eyes and
  his awkwardness,
And remember putting plasters on the galls of his
  neck and ankles;
He staid with me a week before he was recuperated
  and passed north,

I had him sit next me at table .... my firelock leaned
    in the corner.

Twenty-eight young men bathe by the shore,
Twenty-eight young men, and all so friendly,
Twenty-eight years of womanly life, and all so
    lonesome.

She owns the fine house by the rise of the bank,
She hides handsome and richly drest aft the blinds of
    the window.

Which of the young men does she like the best?
Ah the homeliest of them is beautiful to her.

Where are you off to, lady? for I see you,
You splash in the water there, yet stay stock still in
    your room.

Dancing and laughing along the beach came the
    twenty-ninth bather,
The rest did not see her, but she saw them and loved
    them.

The beards of the young men glistened with wet, it
    ran from their long hair,
Little streams passed all over their bodies.

An unseen hand also passed over their bodies,
It descended tremblingly from their temples and ribs.

The young men float on their backs, their white
    bellies swell to the sun .... they do not ask who
    seizes fast to them,
They do not know who puffs and declines with
    pendant and bending arch,
They do not think whom they souse with spray.

The butcher-boy puts off his killing-clothes, or
    sharpens his knife at the stall in the market,
I loiter enjoying his repartee and his shuffle and
    breakdown.
Blacksmiths with grimed and hairy chests environ the
    anvil,
Each has his main-sledge .... they are all out .... there
    is a great heat in the fire.

From the cinder-strewed threshold I follow their
    movements,
The lithe sheer of their waists plays even with their
    massive arms,
Overhand the hammers roll – overhand so slow –
    overhand so sure,
They do not hasten, each man hits in his place.

The negro holds firmly the reins of his four horses ....
    the block swags underneath on its tied-over chain,
The negro that drives the huge dray of the stoneyard
    .... steady and tall he stands poised on one leg on
    the stringpiece,
His blue shirt exposes his ample neck and breast and
    loosens over his hipband,
His glance is calm and commanding .... he tosses the
    slouch of his hat away from his forehead,
The sun falls on his crispy hair and moustache ....
    falls on the black of his polish'd and perfect limbs.

I behold the picturesque giant and love him .... and I
    do not stop there,
I go with the team also.

In me the caresser of life wherever moving ....
    backward as well as forward slueing,
To niches aside and junior bending.

Oxen that rattle the yoke or halt in the shade, what is
    that you express in your eyes?
It seems to me more than all the print I have read in
    my life.

My tread scares the wood-drake and wood-duck on
    my distant and daylong ramble,
They rise together, they slowly circle around.
.... I believe in those winged purposes,
And acknowledge the red yellow and white playing
    within me,
And consider the green and violet and the tufted
    crown intentional;
And do not call the tortoise unworthy because she is
    not something else,
And the mockingbird in the swamp never studied the
    gamut, yet trills pretty well to me,
And the look of the bay mare shames silliness out of
    me.

The wild gander leads his flock through the cool
    night,
Ya-honk! he says, and sounds it down to me like an
    invitation;
The pert may suppose it meaningless, but I listen
    closer,
I find its purpose and place up there toward the
    November sky.

The sharphoofed moose of the north, the cat on the
    housesill, the chickadee, the prairie-dog,
The litter of the grunting sow as they tug at her teats,

The brood of the turkeyhen, and she with her
    halfspread wings,
I see in them and myself the same old law.

The press of my foot to the earth springs a hundred
    affections,
They scorn the best I can do to relate them.

I am enamoured of growing outdoors,
Of men that live among cattle or taste of the ocean or
    woods,
Of the builders and steerers of ships, of the wielders
    of axes and mauls, of the drivers of horses,
I can eat and sleep with them week in and week out.

What is commonest and cheapest and nearest and
    easiest is Me,
Me going in for my chances, spending for vast
    returns,
Adorning myself to bestow myself on the first that
    will take me,
Not asking the sky to come down to my goodwill,
Scattering it freely forever.

The pure contralto sings in the organloft,
The carpenter dresses his plank .... the tongue of his
    foreplane whistles its wild ascending lisp,

The married and unmarried children ride home to
    their thanksgiving dinner,
The pilot seizes the king-pin, he heaves down with a
    strong arm,
The mate stands braced in the whaleboat, lance and
    harpoon are ready,
The duck-shooter walks by silent and cautious
    stretches,
The deacons are ordained with crossed hands at the
    altar,
The spinning-girl retreats and advances to the hum of
    the big wheel,
The farmer stops by the bars of a Sunday and looks at
    the oats and rye,
The lunatic is carried at last to the asylum a
    confirmed case,
He will never sleep any more as he did in the cot in
    his mother's bedroom;
The jour printer with gray head and gaunt jaws works
    at his case,
He turns his quid of tobacco, his eyes get blurred
    with the manuscript;
The malformed limbs are tied to the anatomist's
    table,
What is removed drops horribly in a pail;
The quadroon girl is sold at the stand .... the
    drunkard nods by the barroom stove,

The machinist rolls up his sleeves .... the policeman
    travels his beat .... the gatekeeper marks who pass,
The young fellow drives the express-wagon .... I love
    him though I do not know him;
The half-breed straps on his light boots to compete in
    the race,
The western turkey-shooting draws old and young
    .... some lean on their rifles some sit on logs,
Out from the crowd steps the marksman and takes his
    position and levels his piece;
The groups of newly-come immigrants cover the
    wharf or levee,
The woollypates hoe in the sugarfield, the overseer
    views them from his saddle;
The bugle calls in the ballroom, the gentlemen run
    for their partners, the dancers bow to each other;
The youth lies awake in the cedar-roofed garret and
    harks to the musical rain,
The Wolverine sets traps on the creek that helps fill
    the Huron,
The reformer ascends the platform, he spouts with
    his mouth and nose,
The company returns from its excursion, the darkey
    brings up the rear and bears the well-riddled
    target,
The squaw wrapt in her yellow-hemmed cloth is
    offering moccasins and beadbags for sale,

The connoisseur peers along the exhibition-gallery
    with halfshut eyes bent sideways,
The deckhands make fast the steamboat, the plank is
    thrown for the shoregoing passengers,
The young sister holds out the skein, the elder sister
    winds it off in a ball and stops now and then for the
    knots,
The one-year wife is recovering and happy, a week
    ago she bore her first child,
The cleanhaired Yankee girl works with her
    sewing-machine or in the factory or mill,
The nine months' gone is in the parturition chamber,
    her faintness and pains are advancing;
The pavingman leans on his twohanded rammer – the
    reporter's lead flies swiftly over the notebook – the
    signpainter is lettering with red and gold,
The canal-boy trots on the towpath – the bookkeeper
    counts at his desk – the shoemaker waxes his
    thread,
The conductor beats time for the band and all the
    performers follow him,
The child is baptised – the convert is making the first
    professions,
The regatta is spread on the bay .... how the white
    sails sparkle!
The drover watches his drove, he sings out to them
    that would stray,

The pedlar sweats with his pack on his back – the
    purchaser higgles about the odd cent,
The camera and plate are prepared, the lady must sit
    for her daguerreotype,
The bride unrumples her white dress, the
    minutehand of the clock moves slowly,
The opium eater reclines with rigid head and
    just-opened lips,
The prostitute draggles her shawl, her bonnet bobs
    on her tipsy and pimpled neck,
The crowd laugh at her blackguard oaths, the men
    jeer and wink to each other,
(Miserable! I do not laugh at your oaths nor jeer you,)
The President holds a cabinet council, he is
    surrounded by the great secretaries,
On the piazza walk five friendly matrons with twined
    arms;
The crew of the fish-smack pack repeated layers of
    halibut in the hold,
The Missourian crosses the plains toting his wares
    and his cattle,
The fare-collector goes through the train – he gives
    notice by the jingling of loose change,
The floormen are laying the floor – the tinners are
    tinning the roof – the masons are calling for mortar,
In single file each shouldering his hod pass onward
    the laborers;

Seasons pursuing each other the indescribable crowd
    is gathered .... it is the Fourth of July .... what
    salutes of cannon and small arms!
Seasons pursuing each other the plougher ploughs
    and the mower mows and the wintergrain falls in
    the ground;
Off on the lakes the pikefisher watches and waits by
    the hole in the frozen surface,
The stumps stand thick round the clearing, the
    squatter strikes deep with his axe,
The flatboatmen make fast toward dusk near the
    cottonwood or pekantrees,
The coon-seekers go now through the regions of the
    Red river, or through those drained by the
    Tennessee, or through those of the Arkansas,
The torches shine in the dark that hangs on the
    Chattahoochee or Altamahaw;
Patriarchs sit at supper with sons and grandsons and
    great grandsons around them,
In walls of adobe, in canvass tents, rest hunters and
    trappers after their day's sport.
The city sleeps and the country sleeps,
The living sleep for their time .... the dead sleep for
    their time,
The old husband sleeps by his wife and the young
    husband sleeps by his wife;

And these one and all tend inward to me, and I tend
    outward to them,
And such as it is to be of these more or less I am.

I am of old and young, of the foolish as much as the
    wise,
Regardless of others, ever regardful of others,
Maternal as well as paternal, a child as well as a man,
Stuffed with the stuff that is coarse, and stuffed with
    the stuff that is fine,
One of the great nation, the nation of many nations –
    the smallest the same and the largest the same,
A southerner soon as a northerner, a planter
    nonchalant and hospitable,
A Yankee bound my own way .... ready for trade ....
    my joints the limberest joints on earth and the
    sternest joints on earth,
A Kentuckian walking the vale of the Elkhorn in my
    deerskin leggings,
A boatman over the lakes or bays or along coasts .... a
    Hoosier, a Badger, a Buckeye,
A Louisianian or Georgian, a poke-easy from
    sandhills and pines,
At home on Canadian snowshoes or up in the bush, or
    with fishermen off Newfoundland,
At home in the fleet of iceboats, sailing with the rest
    and tacking,

At home on the hills of Vermont or in the woods of
    Maine or the Texan ranch,
Comrade of Californians .... comrade of free
    northwesterners, loving their big proportions,
Comrade of raftsmen and coalmen – comrade of all
    who shake hands and welcome to drink and meat;
A learner with the simplest, a teacher of the
    thoughtfulest,
A novice beginning experient of myriads of seasons,
Of every hue and trade and rank, of every caste and
    religion,
Not merely of the New World but of Africa Europe
    or Asia .... a wandering savage,
A farmer, mechanic, or artist .... a gentleman, sailor,
    lover or quaker,
A prisoner, fancy-man, rowdy, lawyer, physician or
    priest.

I resist anything better than my own diversity,
And breathe the air and leave plenty after me,
And am not stuck up, and am in my place.

The moth and the fisheggs are in their place,
The suns I see and the suns I cannot see are in their
    place,
The palpable is in its place and the impalpable is in its
    place.

These are the thoughts of all men in all ages and
    lands, they are not original with me,
If they are not yours as much as mine they are
    nothing or next to nothing,
If they do not enclose everything they are next to
    nothing,
If they are not the riddle and the untying of the riddle
    they are nothing,
If they are not just as close as they are distant they are
    nothing.

This is the grass that grows wherever the land is and
    the water is,
This is the common air that bathes the globe.

This is the breath of laws and songs and behaviour,
This is the the tasteless water of souls .... this is the
    true sustenance,
It is for the illiterate .... it is for the judges of the
    supreme court .... it is for the federal capitol and
    the state capitols,
It is for the admirable communes of literary men and
    composers and singers and lecturers and engineers
    and savans,
It is for the endless races of working people and
    farmers and seamen.

This is the trill of a thousand clear cornets and scream
    of the octave flute and strike of triangles.

I play not a march for victors only .... I play great
    marches for conquered and slain persons.

Have you heard that it was good to gain the day?
I also say it is good to fall .... battles are lost in the
    same spirit in which they are won.

I sound triumphal drums for the dead .... I fling
    through my embouchures the loudest and gayest
    music to them,
Vivas to those who have failed, and to those whose
    war-vessels sank in the sea, and those themselves
    who sank in the sea,
And to all generals that lost engagements, and all
    overcome heroes, and the numberless unknown
    heroes equal to the greatest heroes known.

This is the meal pleasantly set .... this is the meat and
    drink for natural hunger,
It is for the wicked just the same as the righteous I
    make appointments with all,
I will not have a single person slighted or left away,

The keptwoman and sponger and thief are hereby
    invited .... the heavy-lipped slave is invited .... the
    venerealee is invited,
There shall be no difference between them and the
    rest.

This is the press of a bashful hand .... this is the float
    and odor of hair,
This is the touch of my lips to yours .... this is the
    murmur of yearning,
This is the far-off depth and height reflecting my own
    face,
This is the thoughtful merge of myself and the outlet
    again.

Do you guess I have some intricate purpose?
Well I have .... for the April rain has, and the mica on
    the side of a rock has.

Do you take it I would astonish?
Does the daylight astonish? or the early redstart
    twittering through the woods?
Do I astonish more than they?

This hour I tell things in confidence,
I might not tell everybody but I will tell you.
fO

Who goes there! hankering, gross, mystical, nude?
How is it I extract strength from the beef I eat?

What is a man anyhow? What am I? and what are
    you?
All I mark as my own you shall offset it with your
    own,
Else it were time lost listening to me.

I do not snivel that snivel the world over,
That months are vacuums and the ground but wallow
    and filth,
That life is a suck and a sell, and nothing remains at
    the end but threadbare crape and tears.

Whimpering and truckling fold with powders for
    invalids .... conformity goes to the fourth-removed,
I cock my hat as I please indoors or out.

Shall I pray? Shall I venerate and be ceremonious?

I have pried through the strata and analyzed to a hair,
And counselled with doctors and calculated close and
    found no sweeter fat than sticks to my own bones.

In all people I see myself, none more and not one a
    barleycorn less,

And the good or bad I say of myself I say of them.

And I know I am solid and sound,
To me the converging objects of the universe
    perpetually flow,
All are written to me, and I must get what the writing
    means.

And I know I am deathless,
I know this orbit of mine cannot be swept by a
    carpenter's compass,
I know I shall not pass like a child's carlacue cut with
    a burnt stick at night.

I know I am august,
I do not trouble my spirit to vindicate itself or be
    understood,
I see that the elementary laws never apologize,
I reckon I behave no prouder than the level I plant
    my house by after all.

I exist as I am, that is enough,
If no other in the world be aware I sit content,
And if each and all be aware I sit content.

One world is aware, and by far the largest to me, and
    that is myself,

And whether I come to my own today or in ten
    thousand or ten million years,
I can cheerfully take it now, or with equal
    cheerfulness I can wait.

My foothold is tenoned and mortised in granite,
I laugh at what you call dissolution,
And I know the amplitude of time.

I am the poet of the body,
And I am the poet of the soul.

The pleasures of heaven are with me, and the pains of
    hell are with me,
The first I graft and increase upon myself .... the
    latter I translate into a new tongue.

I am the poet of the woman the same as the man,
And I say it is as great to be a woman as to be a man,
And I say there is nothing greater than the mother of
    men.
I chant a new chant of dilation or pride,
We have had ducking and deprecating about enough,
I show that size is only developement.

Have you outstript the rest? Are you the President?

It is a trifle .... they will more than arrive there every
    one, and still pass on.

I am he that walks with the tender and growing night;
I call to the earth and sea half-held by the night.

Press close barebosomed night! Press close magnetic
    nourishing night!
Night of south winds! Night of the large few stars!
Still nodding night! Mad naked summer night!

Smile O voluptuous coolbreathed earth!
Earth of the slumbering and liquid trees!
Earth of departed sunset! Earth of the mountains
    misty-topt!
Earth of the vitreous pour of the full moon just tinged
    with blue!
Earth of shine and dark mottling the tide of the river!
Earth of the limpid gray of clouds brighter and
    clearer for my sake!
Far-swooping elbowed earth! Rich apple-blossomed
    earth!
Smile, for your lover comes!

Prodigal! you have given me love! .... therefore I to
    you give love!
O unspeakable passionate love!

Thruster holding me tight and that I hold tight!
We hurt each other as the bridegroom and the bride
    hurt each other.

You sea! I resign myself to you also .... I guess what
    you mean,
I behold from the beach your crooked inviting
    fingers,
I believe you refuse to go back without feeling of me;
We must have a turn together .... I undress .... hurry
    me out of sight of the land,
Cushion me soft .... rock me in billowy drowse,
Dash me with amorous wet .... I can repay you.

Sea of stretched ground-swells!
Sea breathing broad and convulsive breaths!
Sea of the brine of life! Sea of unshovelled and
    always-ready graves!
Howler and scooper of storms! Capricious and dainty
    sea!
I am integral with you .... I too am of one phase and
    of all phases.

Partaker of influx and efflux .... extoler of hate and
    conciliation,

Extoler of amies and those that sleep in each others'
    arms.

I am he attesting sympathy;
Shall I make my list of things in the house and skip
    the house that supports them?

I am the poet of commonsense and of the
    demonstrable and of immortality;
And am not the poet of goodness only .... I do not
    decline to be the poet of wickedness also.

Washes and razors for foofoos .... for me freckles and
    a bristling beard.

What blurt is it about virtue and about vice?
Evil propels me, and reform of evil propels me I
    stand indifferent,
My gait is no faultfinder's or rejecter's gait,
I moisten the roots of all that has grown.

Did you fear some scrofula out of the unflagging
    pregnancy?
Did you guess the celestial laws are yet to be worked
    over and rectified?

I step up to say that what we do is right and what we
    affirm is right .... and some is only the ore of right,
Witnesses of us .... one side a balance and the
    antipodal side a balance,
Soft doctrine as steady help as stable doctrine,
Thoughts and deeds of the present our rouse and
    early start.

This minute that comes to me over the past
    decillions,
There is no better than it and now.

What behaved well in the past or behaves well today
    is not such a wonder,
The wonder is always and always how there can be a
    mean man or an infidel.

Endless unfolding of words of ages!
And mine a word of the modern .... a word en masse.

A word of the faith that never balks,
One time as good as another time .... here or
    henceforward it is all the same to me.

A word of reality .... materialism first and last
    imbueing.

Hurrah for positive science! Long live exact
      demonstration!
Fetch stonecrop and mix it with cedar and branches
      of lilac;
This is the lexicographer or chemist .... this made a
      grammar of the old cartouches,
These mariners put the ship through dangerous
      unknown seas,
This is the geologist, and this works with the scalpel,
      and this is a mathematician.

Gentlemen I receive you, and attach and clasp hands
      with you,
The facts are useful and real .... they are not my
      dwelling .... I enter by them to an area of the
      dwelling.

I am less the reminder of property or qualities, and
      more the reminder of life,
And go on the square for my own sake and for others'
      sakes,
And make short account of neuters and geldings, and
      favor men and women fully equipped,
And beat the gong of revolt, and stop with fugitives
      and them that plot and conspire.

Walt Whitman, an American, one of the roughs, a
    kosmos,
Disorderly fleshy and sensual .... eating drinking and
    breeding,
No sentimentalist .... no stander above men and
    women or apart from them .... no more modest
    than immodest.

Unscrew the locks from the doors!
Unscrew the doors themselves from their jambs!

Whoever degrades another degrades me .... and
    whatever is done or said returns at last to me,
And whatever I do or say I also return.

Through me the afflatus surging and surging ....
    through me the current and index.

I speak the password primeval .... I give the sign of
    democracy;
By God! I will accept nothing which all cannot have
    their counterpart of on the same terms.

Through me many long dumb voices,
Voices of the interminable generations of slaves,
Voices of prostitutes and of deformed persons,

Voices of the diseased and despairing, and of thieves
    and dwarfs,
Voices of cycles of preparation and accretion,
And of the threads that connect the stars – and of
    wombs, and of the fatherstuff,
And of the rights of them the others are down upon,
Of the trivial and flat and foolish and despised,
Of fog in the air and beetles rolling balls of dung.

Through me forbidden voices,
Voices of sexes and lusts …. voices veiled, and I
    remove the veil,
Voices indecent by me clarified and transfigured.
I do not press my finger across my mouth,
I keep as delicate around the bowels as around the
    head and heart,
Copulation is no more rank to me than death is.

I believe in the flesh and the appetites,
Seeing hearing and feeling are miracles, and each part
    and tag of me is a miracle.

Divine am I inside and out, and I make holy whatever
    I touch or am touched from;
The scent of these arm-pits is aroma finer than
    prayer,
This head is more than churches or bibles or creeds.

If I worship any particular thing it shall be some of
  the spread of my body;
Translucent mould of me it shall be you,
Shaded ledges and rests, firm masculine coulter, it
  shall be you,
Whatever goes to the tilth of me it shall be you,
You my rich blood, your milky stream pale strippings
  of my life;
Breast that presses against other breasts it shall be
  you.
My brain it shall be your occult convolutions,
Root of washed sweet-flag, timorous pond-snipe, nest
  of guarded duplicate eggs, it shall be you,
Mixed tussled hay of head and beard and brawn it
  shall be you,
Trickling sap of maple, fibre of manly wheat, it shall
  be you;
Sun so generous it shall be you,
Vapors lighting and shading my face it shall be you,
You sweaty brooks and dews it shall be you,
Winds whose soft-tickling genitals rub against me it
  shall be you,
Broad muscular fields, branches of liveoak, loving
  lounger in my winding paths, it shall be you,
Hands I have taken, face I have kissed, mortal I have
  ever touched, it shall be you.

I dote on myself .... there is that lot of me, and all so
    luscious,
Each moment and whatever happens thrills me with
    joy.
I cannot tell how my ankles bend .... nor whence the
    cause of my faintest wish,
Nor the cause of the friendship I emit .... nor the
    cause of the friendship I take again.

To walk up my stoop is unaccountable .... I pause to
    consider if it really be,
That I eat and drink is spectacle enough for the great
    authors and schools,
A morning-glory at my window satisfies me more
    than the metaphysics of books.

To behold the daybreak!
The little light fades the immense and diaphanous
    shadows,
The air tastes good to my palate.

Hefts of the moving world at innocent gambols,
    silently rising, freshly exuding,
Scooting obliquely high and low.

Something I cannot see puts upward libidinous
    prongs,
Seas of bright juice suffuse heaven.

The earth by the sky staid with .... the daily close of
    their junction,
The heaved challenge from the east that moment over
    my head,
The mocking taunt, See then whether you shall be
    master!

Dazzling and tremendous how quick the sunrise
    would kill me,
If I could not now and always send sunrise out of me.

We also ascend dazzling and tremendous as the sun,
We found our own my soul in the calm and cool of
    the daybreak.

My voice goes after what my eyes cannot reach,
With the twirl of my tongue I encompass worlds and
    volumes of worlds.
Speech is the twin of my vision .... it is unequal to
    measure itself.

It provokes me forever,

It says sarcastically, Walt, you understand enough .... why don't you let it out then?

Come now I will not be tantalized .... you conceive too much of articulation.

Do you not know how the buds beneath are folded?
Waiting in gloom protected by frost,
The dirt receding before my prophetical screams,
I underlying causes to balance them at last,
My knowledge my live parts .... it keeping tally with the meaning of things,
Happiness .... which whoever hears me let him or her set out in search of this day.

My final merit I refuse you .... I refuse putting from me the best I am.

Encompass worlds but never try to encompass me,
I crowd your noisiest talk by looking toward you.

Writing and talk do not prove me,
I carry the plenum of proof and every thing else in my face,
With the hush of my lips I confound the topmost skeptic.

I think I will do nothing for a long time but listen,
And accrue what I hear into myself .... and let sounds
    contribute toward me.

I hear the bravuras of birds .... the bustle of growing
    wheat .... gossip of flames .... clack of sticks
    cooking my meals.

I hear the sound of the human voice .... a sound I
    love,
I hear all sounds as they are tuned to their uses ....
    sounds of the city and sounds out of the city ....
    sounds of the day and night;
Talkative young ones to those that like them .... the
    recitative of fish-pedlars and
fruit-pedlars .... the loud laugh of workpeople at their
    meals,
The angry base of disjointed friendship .... the faint
    tones of the sick,
The judge with hands tight to the desk, his shaky lips
    pronouncing a death-sentence,
The heave'e'yo of stevedores unlading ships by the
    wharves .... the refrain of the anchor-lifters;
The ring of alarm-bells .... the cry of fire .... the
    whirr of swift-streaking engines and hose-carts
    with premonitory tinkles and colored lights,

The steam-whistle .... the solid roll of the train of
    approaching cars;
The slow-march played at night at the head of the
    association,
They go to guard some corpse .... the flag-tops are
    draped with black muslin.

I hear the violincello or man's heart's complaint,
And hear the keyed cornet or else the echo of sunset.

I hear the chorus .... it is a grand-opera .... this
    indeed is music!

A tenor large and fresh as the creation fills me,
The orbic flex of his mouth is pouring and filling me
    full.

I hear the trained soprano .... she convulses me like
    the climax of my love-grip;
The orchestra whirls me wider than Uranus flies,
It wrenches unnamable ardors from my breast,
It throbs me to gulps of the farthest down horror,
It sails me .... I dab with bare feet .... they are licked
    by the indolent waves,
I am exposed .... cut by bitter and poisoned hail,
Steeped amid honeyed morphine .... my windpipe
    squeezed in the fakes of death,

Let up again to feel the puzzle of puzzles,
And that we call Being.

To be in any form, what is that?
If nothing lay more developed the quahaug and its
     callous shell were enough.

Mine is no callous shell,
I have instant conductors all over me whether I pass
     or stop,
They seize every object and lead it harmlessly
     through me.

I merely stir, press, feel with my fingers, and am
     happy,
To touch my person to some one else's is about as
     much as I can stand.

Is this then a touch? .... quivering me to a new
     identity,
Flames and ether making a rush for my veins,
Treacherous tip of me reaching and crowding to help
     them,
My flesh and blood playing out lightning, to strike
     what is hardly different from myself,
On all sides prurient provokers stiffening my limbs,
Straining the udder of my heart for its withheld drip,

Behaving licentious toward me, taking no denial,
Depriving me of my best as for a purpose,
Unbuttoning my clothes and holding me by the bare
    waist,
Deluding my confusion with the calm of the sunlight
    and pasture fields,
Immodestly sliding the fellow-senses away,
They bribed to swap off with touch, and go and graze
    at the edges of me,
No consideration, no regard for my draining strength
    or my anger,
Fetching the rest of the herd around to enjoy them
    awhile,
Then all uniting to stand on a headland and worry
    me.

The sentries desert every other part of me,
They have left me helpless to a red marauder,
They all come to the headland to witness and assist
    against me.
I am given up by traitors;
I talk wildly .... I have lost my wits .... I and nobody
    else am the greatest traitor,
I went myself first to the headland .... my own hands
    carried me there.

You villain touch! what are you doing? .... my breath
   is tight in its throat;
Unclench your floodgates! you are too much for me.

Blind loving wrestling touch! Sheathed hooded
   sharptoothed touch!
Did it make you ache so leaving me?

Parting tracked by arriving .... perpetual payment of
   the perpetual loan,
Rich showering rain, and recompense richer
   afterward.

Sprouts take and accumulate .... stand by the curb
   prolific and vital,
Landscapes projected masculine full-sized and
   golden.

All truths wait in all things,
They neither hasten their own delivery nor resist it,
They do not need the obstetric forceps of the
   surgeon,
The insignificant is as big to me as any,
What is less or more than a touch?

Logic and sermons never convince,
The damp of the night drives deeper into my soul.

Only what proves itself to every man and woman is
    so,
Only what nobody denies is so.

A minute and a drop of me settle my brain;
I believe the soggy clods shall become lovers and
    lamps,
And a compend of compends is the meat of a man or
    woman,
And a summit and flower there is the feeling they
    have for each other,
And they are to branch boundlessly out of that lesson
    until it becomes omnific,
And until every one shall delight us, and we them.

I believe a leaf of grass is no less than the
    journeywork of the stars,
And the pismire is equally perfect, and a grain of
    sand, and the egg of the wren,
And the tree-toad is a chef-d'ouvre for the highest,
And the running blackberry would adorn the parlors
    of heaven,
And the narrowest hinge in my hand puts to scorn all
    machinery,
And the cow crunching with depressed head
    surpasses any statue,

And a mouse is miracle enough to stagger sextillions
    of infidels,
And I could come every afternoon of my life to look
    at the farmer's girl boiling her iron tea-kettle and
    baking shortcake.

I find I incorporate gneiss and coal and long-threaded
    moss and fruits and grains and esculent roots,
And am stucco'd with quadrupeds and birds all over,
And have distanced what is behind me for good
    reasons,
And call any thing close again when I desire it.

In vain the speeding or shyness,
In vain the plutonic rocks send their old heat against
    my approach,
In vain the mastadon retreats beneath its own
    powdered bones,
In vain objects stand leagues off and assume manifold
    shapes,
In vain the ocean settling in hollows and the great
    monsters lying low,
In vain the buzzard houses herself with the sky,
In vain the snake slides through the creepers and logs,
In vain the elk takes to the inner passes of the woods,
In vain the razorbilled auk sails far north to Labrador,

I follow quickly .... I ascend to the nest in the fissure
    of the cliff.

I think I could turn and live awhile with the animals
    .... they are so placid and self-contained,
I stand and look at them sometimes half the day long.

They do not sweat and whine about their condition,
They do not lie awake in the dark and weep for their
    sins,
They do not make me sick discussing their duty to
    God,
Not one is dissatisfied .... not one is demented with
    the mania of owning things,
Not one kneels to another nor to his kind that lived
    thousands of years ago,
Not one is respectable or industrious over the whole
    earth.

So they show their relations to me and I accept them;
They bring me tokens of myself .... they evince them
    plainly in their possession.

I do not know where they got those tokens,
I must have passed that way untold times ago and
    negligently dropt them,
Myself moving forward then and now and forever,

Gathering and showing more always and with
    velocity,
Infinite and omnigenous and the like of these among
    them;
Not too exclusive toward the reachers of my
    remembrancers,
Picking out here one that shall be my amie,
Choosing to go with him on brotherly terms.

A gigantic beauty of a stallion, fresh and responsive to
    my caresses,
Head high in the forehead and wide between the ears,
Limbs glossy and supple, tail dusting the ground,
Eyes well apart and full of sparkling wickedness ....
    ears finely cut and flexibly moving.

His nostrils dilate .... my heels embrace him .... his
    well built limbs tremble with pleasure .... we speed
    around and return.
I but use you a moment and then I resign you stallion
    .... and do not need your paces, and outgallop
    them,
And myself as I stand or sit pass faster than you.

Swift wind! Space! My Soul! Now I know it is true
    what I guessed at;
What I guessed when I loafed on the grass,

What I guessed while I lay alone in my bed .... and
   again as I walked the beach under the paling stars
   of the morning.

My ties and ballasts leave me .... I travel .... I sail ....
   my elbows rest in the sea-gaps,
I skirt the sierras .... my palms cover continents,
I am afoot with my vision.

By the city's quadrangular houses .... in log-huts, or
   camping with lumbermen,
Along the ruts of the turnpike .... along the dry gulch
   and rivulet bed,
Hoeing my onion-patch, and rows of carrots and
   parsnips .... crossing savannas ... trailing in forests,
Prospecting .... gold-digging .... girdling the trees of
   a new purchase,
Scorched ankle-deep by the hot sand .... hauling my
   boat down the shallow river;
Where the panther walks to and fro on a limb
   overhead .... where the buck turns furiously at the
   hunter,
Where the rattlesnake suns his flabby length on a
   rock .... where the otter is feeding on fish,
Where the alligator in his tough pimples sleeps by the
   bayou,

Where the black bear is searching for roots or honey
    .... where the beaver pats the mud with his
    paddle-tail;
Over the growing sugar .... over the cottonplant ....
    over the rice in its low moist field;
Over the sharp-peaked farmhouse with its scalloped
    scum and slender shoots from the gutters;
Over the western persimmon .... over the longleaved
    corn and the delicate blue-flowered flax;
Over the white and brown buckwheat, a hummer and
    a buzzer there with the rest,
Over the dusky green of the rye as it ripples and
    shades in the breeze;
Scaling mountains .... pulling myself cautiously up ....
    holding on by low scragged limbs,
Walking the path worn in the grass and beat through
    the leaves of the brush;
Where the quail is whistling betwixt the woods and
    the wheatlot,
Where the bat flies in the July eve .... where the great
    goldbug drops through the dark;
Where the flails keep time on the barn floor,
Where the brook puts out of the roots of the old tree
    and flows to the meadow,
Where cattle stand and shake away flies with the
    tremulous shuddering of their hides,

Where the cheese-cloth hangs in the kitchen, and
andirons straddle the hearth-slab, and cobwebs fall
in festoons from the rafters;
Where triphammers crash .... where the press is
whirling its cylinders;
Wherever the human heart beats with terrible throes
out of its ribs;
Where the pear-shaped balloon is floating aloft ....
floating in it myself and looking composedly down;
Where the life-car is drawn on the slipnoose ....
where the heat hatches palegreen eggs in the dented
sand,
Where the she-whale swims with her calves and
never forsakes them,
Where the steamship trails hindways its long pennant
of smoke,
Where the ground-shark's fin cuts like a black chip
out of the water,
Where the half-burned brig is riding on unknown
currents,
Where shells grow to her slimy deck, and the dead
are corrupting below;
Where the striped and starred flag is borne at the
head of the regiments;
Approaching Manhattan, up by the long-stretching
island,

Under Niagara, the cataract falling like a veil over my
   countenance;
Upon a door-step .... upon the horse-block of hard
   wood outside,
Upon the race-course, or enjoying pic-nics or jigs or a
   good game of base-ball,
At he-festivals with blackguard jibes and ironical
   license and bull-dances and drinking and laughter,
At the cider-mill, tasting the sweet of the brown
   sqush .... sucking the juice through a straw,
At apple-pealings, wanting kisses for all the red fruit I
   find,
At musters and beach-parties and friendly bees and
   huskings and house-raisings;
Where the mockingbird sounds his delicious gurgles,
   and cackles and screams and weeps,
Where the hay-rick stands in the barnyard, and the
   dry-stalks are scattered, and the brood cow waits in
   the hovel,
Where the bull advances to do his masculine work,
   and the stud to the mare, and the cock is treading
   the hen,
Where the heifers browse, and the geese nip their
   food with short jerks;
Where the sundown shadows lengthen over the
   limitless and lonesome prairie,

Where the herds of buffalo make a crawling spread of
  the square miles far and near;
Where the hummingbird shimmers .... where the
  neck of the longlived swan is curving and winding;
Where the laughing-gull scoots by the slappy shore
  and laughs her near-human laugh;
Where beehives range on a gray bench in the garden
  half- hid by the high weeds;
Where the band-necked partridges roost in a ring on
  the ground with their heads out;
Where burial coaches enter the arched gates of a
  cemetery;
Where winter wolves bark amid wastes of snow and
  icicled trees;
Where the yellow-crowned heron comes to the edge
  of the marsh at night and feeds upon small crabs;
Where the splash of swimmers and divers cools the
  warm noon;
Where the katydid works her chromatic reed on the
  walnut-tree over the well;
Through patches of citrons and cucumbers with
  silver-wired leaves,
Through the salt-lick or orange glade .... or under
  conical furs;
Through the gymnasium .... through the curtained
  saloon .... through the office or public hall;

Pleased with the native and pleased with the foreign
    .... pleased with the new and old,
Pleased with women, the homely as well as the
    handsome,
Pleased with the quakeress as she puts off her bonnet
    and talks melodiously,
Pleased with the primitive tunes of the choir of the
    whitewashed church,
Pleased with the earnest words of the sweating
    Methodist preacher, or any preacher .... looking
    seriously at the camp-meeting;
Looking in at the shop-windows in Broadway the
    whole forenoon .... pressing the flesh of my nose to
    the thick plate-glass,
Wandering the same afternoon with my face turned
    up to the clouds;
My right and left arms round the sides of two friends
    and I in the middle;
Coming home with the bearded and dark-cheeked
    bush-boy .... riding behind him at the drape of the
    day;
Far from the settlements studying the print of
    animals' feet, or the moccasin print;
By the cot in the hospital reaching lemonade to a
    feverish patient,
By the coffined corpse when all is still, examining
    with a candle;

Voyaging to every port to dicker and adventure;
Hurrying with the modern crowd, as eager and fickle
 as any,
Hot toward one I hate, ready in my madness to knife
 him;
Solitary at midnight in my back yard, my thoughts
 gone from me a long while,
Walking the old hills of Judea with the beautiful
 gentle god by my side;
Speeding through space .... speeding through heaven
 and the stars,
Speeding amid the seven satellites and the broad ring
 and the diameter of eighty thousand miles,
Speeding with tailed meteors .... throwing fire-balls
 like the rest,
Carrying the crescent child that carries its own full
 mother in its belly;
Storming enjoying planning loving cautioning,
Backing and filling, appearing and disappearing,
I tread day and night such roads.

I visit the orchards of God and look at the spheric
 product,
And look at quintillions ripened, and look at
 quintillions green.

I fly the flight of the fluid and swallowing soul,

My course runs below the soundings of plummets.

I help myself to material and immaterial,
No guard can shut me off, no law can prevent me.

I anchor my ship for a little while only,
My messengers continually cruise away or bring their
    returns to me.

I go hunting polar furs and the seal .... leaping chasms
    with a pike-pointed staff .... clinging to topples of
    brittle and blue.

I ascend to the foretruck .... I take my place late at
    night in the crow's nest .... we sail through the
    arctic sea .... it is plenty light enough,
Through the clear atmosphere I stretch around on the
    wonderful beauty,
The enormous masses of ice pass me and I pass them
    .... the scenery is plain in all directions,
The white-topped mountains point up in the distance
    .... I fling out my fancies toward them;
We are about approaching some great battlefield in
    which we are soon to be engaged,
We pass the colossal outposts of the encampments ....
    we pass with still feet and caution;

Or we are entering by the suburbs some vast and
    ruined city .... the blocks and fallen architecture
    more than all the living cities of the globe.

I am a free companion .... I bivouac by invading
    watchfires.

I turn the bridegroom out of bed and stay with the
    bride myself,
And tighten her all night to my thighs and lips.

My voice is the wife's voice, the screech by the rail of
    the stairs,
They fetch my man's body up dripping and drowned.

I understand the large hearts of heroes,
The courage of present times and all times;
How the skipper saw the crowded and rudderless
    wreck of the steamship, and death chasing it up and
    down the storm,
How he knuckled tight and gave not back one inch,
    and was faithful of days and faithful of nights,
And chalked in large letters on a board, Be of good
    cheer, We will not desert you;
How he saved the drifting company at last,
How the lank loose-gowned women looked when
    boated from the side of their prepared graves,

How the silent old-faced infants, and the lifted sick,
    and the sharp-lipped unshaved men;
All this I swallow and it tastes good .... I like it well,
    and it becomes mine,
I am the man .... I suffered .... I was there.

The disdain and calmness of martyrs,
The mother condemned for a witch and burnt with
    dry wood, and her children gazing on;
The hounded slave that flags in the race and leans by
    the fence, blowing and covered with sweat,
The twinges that sting like needles his legs and neck,
The murderous buckshot and the bullets,
All these I feel or am.

I am the hounded slave .... I wince at the bite of the
    dogs,
Hell and despair are upon me .... crack and again
    crack the marksmen,
I clutch the rails of the fence .... my gore dribs
    thinned with the ooze of my skin,
I fall on the weeds and stones,
The riders spur their unwilling horses and haul close,
They taunt my dizzy ears .... they beat me violently
    over the head with their whip-stocks.

Agonies are one of my changes of garments;

I do not ask the wounded person how he feels I
    myself become the wounded person,
My hurt turns livid upon me as I lean on a cane and
    observe.

I am the mashed fireman with breastbone broken ....
    tumbling walls buried me in their debris,
Heat and smoke I inspired .... I heard the yelling
    shouts of my comrades,
I heard the distant click of their picks and shovels;
They have cleared the beams away .... they tenderly
    lift me forth.

I lie in the night air in my red shirt .... the pervading
    hush is for my sake,
Painless after all I lie, exhausted but not so unhappy,
White and beautiful are the faces around me .... the
    heads are bared of their firecaps,
The kneeling crowd fades with the light of the
    torches.

Distant and dead resuscitate,
They show as the dial or move as the hands of me ....
    and I am the clock myself.
I am an old artillerist, and tell of some fort's
    bombardment .... and am there again.

Again the reveille of drummers .... again the
    attacking cannon and mortars and howitzers,
Again the attacked send their cannon responsive.

I take part .... I see and hear the whole,
The cries and curses and roar .... the plaudits for well
    aimed shots,
The ambulanza slowly passing and trailing its red
    drip,
Workmen searching after damages and to make
    indispensible repairs,
The fall of grenades through the rent roof .... the
    fan-shaped explosion,
The whizz of limbs heads stone wood and iron high in
    the air.

Again gurgles the mouth of my dying general .... he
    furiously waves with his hand,
He gasps through the clot .... Mind not me .... mind
    .... the entrenchments.

I tell not the fall of Alamo .... not one escaped to tell
    the fall of Alamo,
The hundred and fifty are dumb yet at Alamo.

Hear now the tale of a jetblack sunrise,

Hear of the murder in cold blood of four hundred and
    twelve young men.

Retreating they had formed in a hollow square with
    their baggage for breastworks,
Nine hundred lives out of the surrounding enemy's
    nine times their number was the price they took in
    advance,
Their colonel was wounded and their ammunition
    gone,
They treated for an honorable capitulation, received
    writing and seal, gave up their arms, and marched
    back prisoners of war.
They were the glory of the race of rangers,
Matchless with a horse, a rifle, a song, a supper or a
    courtship,
Large, turbulent, brave, handsome, generous, proud
    and affectionate,
Bearded, sunburnt, dressed in the free costume of
    hunters,
Not a single one over thirty years of age.

The second Sunday morning they were brought out
    in squads and massacred …. it was beautiful early
    summer,
The work commenced about five o'clock and was
    over by eight.

None obeyed the command to kneel,
Some made a mad and helpless rush .... some stood
    stark and straight,
A few fell at once, shot in the temple or heart .... the
    living and dead lay together,
The maimed and mangled dug in the dirt .... the
    new- comers saw them there;
Some half-killed attempted to crawl away,
These were dispatched with bayonets or battered
    with the blunts of muskets;
A youth not seventeen years old seized his assassin till
    two more came to release him,
The three were all torn, and covered with the boy's
    blood.

At eleven o'clock began the burning of the bodies;
And that is the tale of the murder of the four hundred
    and twelve young men,
And that was a jetblack sunrise.

Did you read in the seabooks of the oldfashioned
    frigate-fight?
Did you learn who won by the light of the moon and
    stars?

Our foe was no skulk in his ship, I tell you,

His was the English pluck, and there is no tougher or
    truer, and never was, and never will be;
Along the lowered eve he came, horribly raking us.

We closed with him .... the yards entangled .... the
    cannon touched,
My captain lashed fast with his own hands.

We had received some eighteen-pound shots under
    the water,
On our lower-gun-deck two large pieces had burst at
    the first fire, killing all around and blowing up
    overhead.

Ten o'clock at night, and the full moon shining and
    the leaks on the gain, and five feet of water
    reported,
The master-at-arms loosing the prisoners confined in
    the after-hold to give them a chance for themselves.

The transit to and from the magazine was now
    stopped by the sentinels,
They saw so many strange faces they did not know
    whom to trust.

Our frigate was afire .... the other asked if we
  demanded quarters? if our colors were struck and
  the fighting done?

I laughed content when I heard the voice of my little
  captain,
We have not struck, he composedly cried, We have
  just begun our part of the fighting.

Only three guns were in use,
One was directed by the captain himself against the
  enemy's mainmast,
Two well-served with grape and canister silenced his
  musketry and cleared his decks.

The tops alone seconded the fire of this little battery,
  especially the maintop,
They all held out bravely during the whole of the
  action.

Not a moment's cease,
The leaks gained fast on the pumps .... the fire eat
  toward the powder-magazine,
One of the pumps was shot away .,.. it was generally
  thought we were sinking.
Serene stood the little captain,

He was not hurried .... his voice was neither high nor
    low,
His eyes gave more light to us than our
    battle-lanterns.

Toward twelve at night, there in the beams of the
    moon they surrendered to us.

Stretched and still lay the midnight,
Two great hulls motionless on the breast of the
    darkness,
Our vessel riddled and slowly sinking ....
    preparations to pass to the one we had conquered,
The captain on the quarter deck coldly giving his
    orders through a countenance white as a sheet,
Near by the corpse of the child that served in the
    cabin,
The dead face of an old salt with long white hair and
    carefully curled whiskers,
The flames spite of all that could be done flickering
    aloft and below,
The husky voices of the two or three officers yet fit
    for duty,
Formless stacks of bodies and bodies by themselves
    .... dabs of flesh upon the masts and spars,
The cut of cordage and dangle of rigging .... the slight
    shock of the soothe of waves,

Black and impassive guns, and litter of
    powder-parcels, and the strong scent,
Delicate sniffs of the seabreeze .... smells of sedgy
    grass and fields by the shore ... death-messages
    given in charge to survivors,
The hiss of the surgeon's knife and the gnawing teeth
    of his saw,
The wheeze, the cluck, the swash of falling blood ....
    the short wild scream, the long dull tapering groan,
These so .... these irretrievable.

O Christ! My fit is mastering me!
What the rebel said gaily adjusting his throat to the
    rope-noose,
What the savage at the stump, his eye-sockets empty,
    his mouth spirting whoops and defiance,
What stills the traveler come to the vault at Mount
    Vernon,
What sobers the Brooklyn boy as he looks down the
    shores of the Wallabout and remembers the prison
    ships,
What burnt the gums of the redcoat at Saratoga when
    he surrendered his brigades,
These become mine and me every one, and they are
    but little,
I become as much more as I like.
I become any presence or truth of humanity here,

And see myself in prison shaped like another man,
And feel the dull unintermitted pain.

For me the keepers of convicts shoulder their
    carbines and keep watch,
It is I let out in the morning and barred at night.

Not a mutineer walks handcuffed to the jail, but I am
    handcuffed to him and walk by his side,
I am less the jolly one there, and more the silent one
    with sweat on my twitching lips.

Not a youngster is taken for larceny, but I go up too
    and am tried and sentenced.

Not a cholera patient lies at the last gasp, but I also lie
    at the last gasp,
My face is ash-colored, my sinews gnarl .... away
    from me people retreat.

Askers embody themselves in me, and I am embodied
    in them,
I project my hat and sit shamefaced and beg.

I rise extatic through all, and sweep with the true
    gravitation,
The whirling and whirling is elemental within me.

Somehow I have been stunned. Stand back!
Give me a little time beyond my cuffed head and
    slumbers and dreams and gaping,
I discover myself on a verge of the usual mistake.

That I could forget the mockers and insults!
That I could forget the trickling tears and the blows
    of the bludgeons and hammers!
That I could look with a separate look on my own
    crucifixion and bloody crowning!

I remember .... I resume the overstaid fraction,
The grave of rock multiplies what has been confided
    to it .... or to any graves,
The corpses rise .... the gashes heal .... the fastenings
    roll away.

I troop forth replenished with supreme power, one of
    an average unending procession,
We walk the roads of Ohio and Massachusetts and
    Virginia and Wisconsin and New York and New
    Orleans and Texas and Montreal and San Francisco
    and Charleston and Savannah and Mexico,
Inland and by the seacoast and boundary lines .... and
    we pass the boundary lines.

Our swift ordinances are on their way over the whole
    earth,
The blossoms we wear in our hats are the growth of
    two thousand years.

Eleves I salute you,
I see the approach of your numberless gangs .... I see
    you understand yourselves and me,
And know that they who have eyes are divine, and
    the blind and lame are equally divine,
And that my steps drag behind yours yet go before
    them,
And are aware how I am with you no more than I am
    with everybody.

The friendly and flowing savage .... Who is he?
Is he waiting for civilization or past it and mastering
    it?

Is he some southwesterner raised outdoors? Is he
    Canadian?
Is he from the Mississippi country? or from Iowa,
    Oregon or California? or from the mountains? or
    prairie life or bush-life? or from the sea?
Wherever he goes men and women accept and desire
    him,

They desire he should like them and touch them and
    speak to them and stay with them.

Behaviour lawless as snow-flakes .... words simple as
    grass .... uncombed head and laughter and naivete;
Slowstepping feet and the common features, and the
    common modes and emanations,
They descend in new forms from the tips of his
    fingers,
They are wafted with the odor of his body or breath
    .... they fly out of the glance of his eyes.

Flaunt of the sunshine I need not your bask .... lie
    over,
You light surfaces only .... I force the surfaces and the
    depths also.

Earth! you seem to look for something at my hands,
Say old topknot! what do you want?

Man or woman! I might tell how I like you, but
    cannot,
And might tell what it is in me and what it is in you,
    but cannot,
And might tell the pinings I have .... the pulse of my
    nights and days.

Behold I do not give lectures or a little charity,
What I give I give out of myself.

You there, impotent, loose in the knees, open your
    scarfed chops till I blow grit within you,
Spread your palms and lift the flaps of your pockets,
I am not to be denied .... I compel .... I have stores
    plenty and to spare,
And any thing I have I bestow.

I do not ask who you are .... that is not important to
    me,
You can do nothing and be nothing but what I will
    infold you.

To a drudge of the cottonfields or emptier of privies I
    lean .... on his right cheek I put the family kiss,
And in my soul I swear I never will deny him.
On women fit for conception I start bigger and
    nimbler babes,
This day I am jetting the stuff of far more arrogant
    republics.

To any one dying .... thither I speed and twist the
    knob of the door,
Turn the bedclothes toward the foot of the bed,
Let the physician and the priest go home.

I seize the descending man .... I raise him with
    resistless will.

O despairer, here is my neck,
By God! you shall not go down! Hang your whole
    weight upon me.

I dilate you with tremendous breath .... I buoy you
    up;
Every room of the house do I fill with am armed force
    .... lovers of me, bafflers of graves:
Sleep! I and they keep guard all night;
Not doubt, not decease shall dare to lay finger upon
    you,
I have embraced you, and henceforth possess you to
    myself,
And when you rise in the morning you will find what
    I tell you is so.

I am he bringing help for the sick as they pant on
    their backs,
And for strong upright men I bring yet more needed
    help.

I heard what was said of the universe,
Heard it and heard of several thousand years;

It is middling well as far as it goes .... but is that all?

Magnifying and applying come I,
Outbidding at the start the old cautious hucksters,
The most they offer for mankind and eternity less
    than a spirt of my own seminal wet,
Taking myself the exact dimensions of Jehovah and
    laying them away,
Lithographing Kronos and Zeus his son, and
    Hercules his grandson,
Buying drafts of Osiris and Isis and Belus and Brahma
    and Adonai,
In my portfolio placing Manito loose, and Allah on a
    leaf, and the crucifix engraved,
With Odin, and the hideous-faced Mexitli, and all
    idols and images,
Honestly taking them all for what they are worth, and
    not a cent more,
Admitting they were alive and did the work of their
    day,
Admitting they bore mites as for unfledged birds who
    have now to rise and fly and sing for themselves,
Accepting the rough deific sketches to fill out better
    in myself .... bestowing them freely on each man
    and woman I see,
Discovering as much or more in a framer framing a
    house,

Putting higher claims for him there with his rolled-up
    sleeves, driving the mallet and chisel;
Not objecting to special revelations .... considering a
    curl of smoke or a hair on the back of my hand as
    curious as any revelation;
Those ahold of fire-engines and hook-and-ladder
    ropes more to me than the gods of the antique wars,
Minding their voices peal through the crash of
    destruction,
Their brawny limbs passing safe over charred laths
    .... their white foreheads whole and unhurt out of
    the flames;
By the mechanic's wife with her babe at her nipple
    interceding for every person born;
Three scythes at harvest whizzing in a row from three
    lusty angels with shirts bagged out at their waists;
The snag-toothed hostler with red hair redeeming
    sins past and to come,
Selling all he possesses and traveling on foot to fee
    lawyers for his brother and sit by him while he is
    tried for forgery:
What was strewn in the amplest strewing the square
    rod about me, and not filling the square rod then;
The bull and the bug never worshipped half enough,
Dung and dirt more admirable than was dreamed,
The supernatural of no account .... myself waiting my
    time to be one of the supremes,

The day getting ready for me when I shall do as much
    good as the best, and be as prodigious,
Guessing when I am it will not tickle me much to
    receive puffs out of pulpit or print;
By my life-lumps! becoming already a creator!
Putting myself here and now to the ambushed womb
    of the shadows!

.... A call in the midst of the crowd,
My own voice, orotund sweeping and final.

Come my children,
Come my boys and girls, and my women and
    household and intimates,
Now the performer launches his nerve .... he has
    passed his prelude on the reeds within.

Easily written loosefingered chords! I feel the thrum
    of their climax and close.

My head evolves on my neck,
Music rolls, but not from the organ .... folks are
    around me, but they are no household of mine.

Ever the hard and unsunk ground,

Ever the eaters and drinkers .... ever the upward and
  downward sun .... ever the air and the ceaseless
  tides,
Ever myself and my neighbors, refreshing and wicked
  and real,
Ever the old inexplicable query .... ever that thorned
  thumb – that breath of itches and thirsts,
Ever the vexer's hoot! hoot! till we find where the sly
  one hides and bring him forth;
Ever love .... ever the sobbing liquid of life,
Ever the bandage under the chin .... ever the tressels
  of death.

Here and there with dimes on the eyes walking,
To feed the greed of the belly the brains liberally
  spooning,
Tickets buying or taking or selling, but in to the feast
  never once going;
Many sweating and ploughing and thrashing, and
  then the chaff for payment receiving,
A few idly owning, and they the wheat continually
  claiming.

This is the city .... and I am one of the citizens;
Whatever interests the rest interests me .... politics,
  churches, newspapers, schools,

Benevolent societies, improvements, banks, tariffs,
    steamships, factories, markets,
Stocks and stores and real estate and personal estate.

They who piddle and patter here in collars and tailed
    coats .... I am aware who they are .... and that they
    are not worms or fleas,
I acknowledge the duplicates of myself under all the
    scrape-lipped and pipe-legged concealments.

The weakest and shallowest is deathless with me,
What I do and say the same waits for them,
Every thought that flounders in me the same
    flounders in them.

I know perfectly well my own egotism,
And know my omniverous words, and cannot say any
    less,
And would fetch you whoever you are flush with
    myself.

My words are words of a questioning, and to indicate
    reality;
This printed and bound book .... but the printer and
    the printing-office boy?

The marriage estate and settlement .... but the body
    and mind of the bridegroom? also those of the
    bride?
The panorama of the sea .... but the sea itself?
The well-taken photographs .... but your wife or
    friend close and solid in your arms?
The fleet of ships of the line and all the modern
    improvements .... but the craft and pluck of the
    admiral?
The dishes and fare and furniture .... but the host and
    hostess, and the look out of their eyes?
The sky up there .... yet here or next door or across
    the way?
The saints and sages in history .... but you yourself?
Sermons and creeds and theology .... but the human
    brain, and what is called reason, and what is called
    love, and what is called life?

I do not despise you priests;
My faith is the greatest of faiths and the least of faiths,
Enclosing all worship ancient and modern, and all
    between ancient and modern,
Believing I shall come again upon the earth after five
    thousand years,
Waiting responses from oracles .... honoring the gods
    .... saluting the sun,

Making a fetish of the first rock or stump .... powowing with sticks in the circle of obis,
Helping the lama or brahmin as he trims the lamps of the idols,
Dancing yet through the streets in a phallic procession .... rapt and austere in the woods, a gymnosophist,
Drinking mead from the skull-cup .... to shasta and vedas admirant .... minding the koran,
Walking the teokallis, spotted with gore from the stone and knife – beating the serpent-skin drum;
Accepting the gospels, accepting him that was crucified, knowing assuredly that he is divine,
To the mass kneeling – to the puritan's prayer rising – sitting patiently in a pew,
Ranting and frothing in my insane crisis – waiting dead-like till my spirit arouses me;
Looking forth on pavement and land, and outside of pavement and land,
Belonging to the winders of the circuit of circuits.

One of that centripetal and centrifugal gang,
I turn and talk like a man leaving charges before a journey.
Down-hearted doubters, dull and excluded,
Frivolous sullen moping angry affected disheartened atheistical,

I know every one of you, and know the unspoken
    interrogatories,
By experience I know them.

How the flukes splash!
How they contort rapid as lightning, with spasms and
    spouts of blood!

Be at peace bloody flukes of doubters and sullen
    mopers,
I take my place among you as much as among any;
The past is the push of you and me and all precisely
    the same,
And the day and night are for you and me and all,
And what is yet untried and afterward is for you and
    me and all.

I do not know what is untried and afterward,
But I know it is sure and alive, and sufficient.

Each who passes is considered, and each who stops is
    considered, and not a single one can it fail.

It cannot fail the young man who died and was
    buried,
Nor the young woman who died and was put by his
    side,

Nor the little child that peeped in at the door and
   then drew back and was never seen again,
Nor the old man who has lived without purpose, and
   feels it with bitterness worse than gall,
Nor him in the poorhouse tubercled by rum and the
   bad disorder,
Nor the numberless slaughtered and wrecked .... nor
   the brutish koboo, called the ordure of humanity,
Nor the sacs merely floating with open mouths for
   food to slip in,
Nor any thing in the earth, or down in the oldest
   graves of the earth,
Nor any thing in the myriads of spheres, nor one of
   the myriads of myriads that inhabit them,
Nor the present, nor the least wisp that is known.
It is time to explain myself .... let us stand up.

What is known I strip away .... I launch all men and
   women forward with me into the unknown.

The clock indicates the moment .... but what does
   eternity indicate?

Eternity lies in bottomless reservoirs .... its buckets
   are rising forever and ever,
They pour and they pour and they exhale away.

We have thus far exhausted trillions of winters and
  summers;
There are trillions ahead, and trillions ahead of them.

Births have brought us richness and variety,
And other births will bring us richness and variety.

I do not call one greater and one smaller,
That which fills its period and place is equal to any.

Were mankind murderous or jealous upon you my
  brother or my sister?
I am sorry for you .... they are not murderous or
  jealous upon me;
All has been gentle with me ...... I keep no account
  with lamentation;
What have I to do with lamentation?

I am an acme of things accomplished, and I an
  encloser of things to be.

My feet strike an apex of the apices of the stairs,
On every step bunches of ages, and larger bunches
  between the steps,
All below duly traveled – and still I mount and
  mount.

Rise after rise bow the phantoms behind me,
Afar down I see the huge first Nothing, the vapor
    from the nostrils of death,
I know I was even there .... I waited unseen and
    always,
And slept while God carried me through the lethargic
    mist,
And took my time .... and took no hurt from the
    foetid carbon.

Long I was hugged close .... long and long.

Immense have been the preparations for me,
Faithful and friendly the arms that have helped me.

Cycles ferried my cradle, rowing and rowing like
    cheerful boatmen;
For room to me stars kept aside in their own rings,
They sent influences to look after what was to hold
    me.

Before I was born out of my mother generations
    guided me,
My embryo has never been torpid .... nothing could
    overlay it;

For it the nebula cohered to an orb .... the long slow
    strata piled to rest it on .... vast vegetables gave it
    sustenance,
Monstrous sauroids transported it in their mouths
    and deposited it with care.

All forces have been steadily employed to complete
    and delight me,
Now I stand on this spot with my soul.

Span of youth! Ever-pushed elasticity! Manhood
    balanced and florid and full!

My lovers suffocate me!
Crowding my lips, and thick in the pores of my skin,
Jostling me through streets and public halls ....
    coming naked to me at night,
Crying by day Ahoy from the rocks of the river ....
    swinging and chirping over my head,
Calling my name from flowerbeds or vines or tangled
    underbrush,
Or while I swim in the bath .... or drink from the
    pump at the corner .... or the curtain is down at the
    opera .... or I glimpse at a woman's face in the
    railroad car;
Lighting on every moment of my life,
Bussing my body with soft and balsamic busses,

Noiselessly passing handfuls out of their hearts and
  giving them to be mine.

Old age superbly rising! Ineffable grace of dying days!

Every condition promulges not only itself .... it
  promulges what grows after and out of itself,
And the dark hush promulges as much as any.

I open my scuttle at night and see the far-sprinkled
  systems,
And all I see, multiplied as high as I can cipher, edge
  but the rim of the farther systems.

Wider and wider they spread, expanding and always
  expanding,
Outward and outward and forever outward.

My sun has his sun, and round him obediently
  wheels,
He joins with his partners a group of superior circuit,
And greater sets follow, making specks of the greatest
  inside them.

There is no stoppage, and never can be stoppage;
If I and you and the worlds and all beneath or upon
  their surfaces, and all the palpable life, were this

moment reduced back to a pallid float, it would not
  avail in the long run,
We should surely bring up again where we now
  stand,
And as surely go as much farther, and then farther
  and farther.

A few quadrillions of eras, a few octillions of cubic
  leagues, do not hazard the span, or make it
  impatient,
They are but parts .... any thing is but a part.

See ever so far .... there is limitless space outside of
  that,
Count ever so much .... there is limitless time around
  that.
Our rendezvous is fitly appointed .... God will be
  there and wait till we come.

I know I have the best of time and space – and that I
  was never measured, and never will be measured.

I tramp a perpetual journey,
My signs are a rain-proof coat and good shoes and a
  staff cut from the woods;
No friend of mine takes his ease in my chair,
I have no chair, nor church nor philosophy;

I lead no man to a dinner-table or library or
    exchange,
But each man and each woman of you I lead upon a
    knoll,
My left hand hooks you round the waist,
My right hand points to landscapes of continents, and
    a plain public road.

Not I, not any one else can travel that road for you,
You must travel it for yourself.

It is not far .... it is within reach,
Perhaps you have been on it since you were born, and
    did not know,
Perhaps it is every where on water and on land.

Shoulder your duds, and I will mine, and let us hasten
    forth;
Wonderful cities and free nations we shall fetch as we
    go.

If you tire, give me both burdens, and rest the chuff
    of your hand on my hip,
And in due time you shall repay the same service to
    me;
For after we start we never lie by again.

This day before dawn I ascended a hill and looked at
    the crowded heaven,
And I said to my spirit, When we become the
    enfolders of those orbs and the pleasure and
    knowledge of every thing in them, shall we be filled
    and satisfied then?
And my spirit said No, we level that lift to pass and
    continue beyond.
You are also asking me questions, and I hear you;
I answer that I cannot answer .... you must find out
    for yourself.

Sit awhile wayfarer,
Here are biscuits to eat and here is milk to drink,
But as soon as you sleep and renew yourself in sweet
    clothes I will certainly kiss you with my goodbye
    kiss and open the gate for your egress hence.

Long enough have you dreamed contemptible
    dreams,
Now I wash the gum from your eyes,
You must habit yourself to the dazzle of the light and
    of every moment of your life

Long have you timidly waded, holding a plank by the
    shore,
Now I will you to be a bold swimmer,

To jump off in the midst of the sea, and rise again and
    nod to me and shout, and laughingly dash with
    your hair.

I am the teacher of athletes,
He that by me spreads a wider breast than my own
    proves the width of my own,
He most honors my style who learns under it to
    destroy the teacher.

The boy I love, the same becomes a man not through
    derived power but in his own right,
Wicked, rather than virtuous out of conformity or
    fear,
Fond of his sweetheart, relishing well his steak,
Unrequited love or a slight cutting him worse than a
    wound cuts,
First rate to ride, to fight, to hit the bull's eye, to sail
    a skiff, to sing a song or play on the banjo,
Preferring scars and faces pitted with smallpox over
    all latherers and those that keep out of the sun.

I teach straying from me, yet who can stray from me?
I follow you whoever you are from the present hour;
My words itch at your ears till you understand them.
I do not say these things for a dollar, or to fill up the
    time while I wait for a boat;

It is you talking just as much as myself .... I act as the
    tongue of you,
It was tied in your mouth .... in mine it begins to be
    loosened.

I swear I will never mention love or death inside a
    house,
And I swear I never will translate myself at all, only
    to him or her who privately stays with me in the
    open air.

If you would understand me go to the heights or
    water-shore,
The nearest gnat is an explanation and a drop or the
    motion of waves a key,
The maul the oar and the handsaw second my words.

No shuttered room or school can commune with me,
But roughs and little children better than they.

The young mechanic is closest to me .... he knows me
    pretty well,
The woodman that takes his axe and jug with him
    shall take me with him all day,
The farmboy ploughing in the field feels good at the
    sound of my voice,

In vessels that sail my words must sail .... I go with
    fishermen and seamen, and love them,
My face rubs to the hunter's face when he lies down
    alone in his blanket,
The driver thinking of me does not mind the jolt of
    his wagon,
The young mother and old mother shall comprehend
    me,
The girl and the wife rest the needle a moment and
    forget where they are,
They and all would resume what I have told them.

I have said that the soul is not more than the body,
And I have said that the body is not more than the
    soul,
And nothing, not God, is greater to one than
    one's-self is,
And whoever walks a furlong without sympathy
    walks to his own funeral, dressed in his shroud,
And I or you pocketless of a dime may purchase the
    pick of the earth,
And to glance with an eye or show a bean in its pod
    confounds the learning of all times,
And there is no trade or employment but the young
    man following it may become a hero,
And there is no object so soft but it makes a hub for
    the wheeled universe,

And any man or woman shall stand cool and
  supercilious before a million universes.

And I call to mankind, Be not curious about God,
For I who am curious about each am not curious
  about God,
No array of terms can say how much I am at peace
  about God and about death.

I hear and behold God in every object, yet I
  understand God not in the least,
Nor do I understand who there can be more
  wonderful than myself.

Why should I wish to see God better than this day?
I see something of God each hour of the twenty-four,
  and each moment then,
In the faces of men and women I see God, and in my
  own face in the glass;
I find letters from God dropped in the street, and
  every one is signed by God's name,
And I leave them where they are, for I know that
  others will punctually come forever and ever.

And as to you death, and you bitter hug of mortality
  .... it is idle to try to alarm me.

To his work without flinching the accoucheur comes,
I see the elderhand pressing receiving supporting,
I recline by the sills of the exquisite flexible doors ....
    and mark the outlet, and mark the relief and
    escape.
And as to you corpse I think you are good manure,
    but that does not offend me,
I smell the white roses sweetscented and growing,
I reach to the leafy lips .... I reach to the polished
    breasts of melons.

And as to you life, I reckon you are the leavings of
    many deaths,
No doubt I have died myself ten thousand times
    before.

I hear you whispering there O stars of heaven,
O suns .... O grass of graves .... O perpetual transfers
    and promotions .... if you do not say anything how
    can I say anything?

Of the turbid pool that lies in the autumn forest,
Of the moon that descends the steeps of the soughing
    twilight,
Toss, sparkles of day and dusk .... toss on the black
    stems that decay in the muck,
Toss to the moaning gibberish of the dry limbs.

I ascend from the moon .... I ascend from the night,
And perceive of the ghastly glitter the sunbeams
    reflected,
And debouch to the steady and central from the
    offspring great or small.

There is that in me .... I do not know what it is ....
    but I know it is in me.

Wrenched and sweaty .... calm and cool then my
    body becomes;
I sleep .... I sleep long.

I do not know it .... it is without name .... it is a word
    unsaid,
It is not in any dictionary or utterance or symbol.

Something it swings on more than the earth I swing
    on,
To it the creation is the friend whose embracing
    awakes me.
Perhaps I might tell more .... Outlines! I plead for my
    brothers and sisters.

Do you see O my brothers and sisters?

It is not chaos or death .... it is form and union and
    plan .... it is eternal life .... it is happiness.

The past and present wilt .... I have filled them and
    emptied them,
And proceed to fill my next fold of the future.

Listener up there! Here you .... what have you to
    confide to me?
Look in my face while I snuff the sidle of evening,
Talk honestly, for no one else hears you, and I stay
    only a minute longer.

Do I contradict myself?
Very well then .... I contradict myself;
I am large .... I contain multitudes.

I concentrate toward them that are nigh .... I wait on
    the door-slab.

Who has done his day's work and will soonest be
    through with his supper?
Who wishes to walk with me?

Will you speak before I am gone? Will you prove
    already too late?

The spotted hawk swoops by and accuses me .... he
    complains of my gab and my loitering.

I too am not a bit tamed .... I too am untranslatable,
I sound my barbaric yawp over the roofs of the
    world.

The last scud of day holds back for me,
It flings my likeness after the rest and true as any on
    the shadowed wilds,
It coaxes me to the vapor and the dusk.
I depart as air .... I shake my white locks at the
    runaway sun,
I effuse my flesh in eddies and drift it in lacy jags.

I bequeath myself to the dirt to grow from the grass I
    love,
If you want me again look for me under your
    bootsoles.

You will hardly know who I am or what I mean,
But I shall be good health to you nevertheless,
And filter and fibre your blood.

Failing to fetch me me at first keep encouraged,
Missing me one place search another,
I stop some where waiting for you.

The Sleepers

I wander all night in my vision,
Stepping with light feet …. swiftly and noiselessly
    stepping and stopping,
Bending with open eyes over the shut eyes of
    sleepers;
Wandering and confused …. lost to myself ….
    ill-assorted …. contradictory,
Pausing and gazing and bending and stopping.

How solemn they look there, stretched and still;
How quiet they breathe, the little children in their
    cradles.

The wretched features of ennuyees, the white
    features of corpses, the livid faces of drunkards, the
    sick-gray faces of onanists,
The gashed bodies on battlefields, the insane in their
    strong-doored rooms, the sacred idiots,
The newborn emerging from gates and the dying
    emerging from gates,
The night pervades them and enfolds them.

Originally untitled

The married couple sleep calmly in their bed, he with
    his palm on the hip of the wife, and she with her
    palm on the hip of the husband,
The sisters sleep lovingly side by side in their bed,
The men sleep lovingly side by side in theirs,
And the mother sleeps with her little child carefully
    wrapped.

The blind sleep, and the deaf and dumb sleep,
The prisoner sleeps well in the prison .... the
    runaway son sleeps,
The murderer that is to be hung next day .... how
    does he sleep?
And the murdered person .... how does he sleep?

The female that loves unrequited sleeps,
And the male that loves unrequited sleeps;
The head of the moneymaker that plotted all day
    sleeps,
And the enraged and treacherous dispositions sleep.

I stand with drooping eyes by the worstsuffering and
    restless,
I pass my hands soothingly to and fro a few inches
    from them;
The restless sink in their beds .... they fitfully sleep.

The earth recedes from me into the night,
I saw that it was beautiful .... and I see that what is
    not the earth is beautiful.

I go from bedside to bedside .... I sleep close with the
    other sleepers, each in turn;
I dream in my dream all the dreams of the other
    dreamers,
And I become the other dreamers.

I am a dance .... Play up there! the fit is whirling me
    fast.

I am the everlaughing .... it is new moon and
    twilight,
I see the hiding of douceurs .... I see nimble ghosts
    whichever way I look,
Cache and cache again deep in the ground and sea,
    and where it is neither ground or sea.

Well do they do their jobs, those journeymen divine,
Only from me can they hide nothing and would not if
    they could;
I reckon I am their boss, and they make me a pet
    besides,
And surround me, and lead me and run ahead when I
    walk,

And lift their cunning covers and signify me with
    stretched arms, and resume the way;
Onward we move, a gay gang of blackguards with
    mirthshouting music and wild-flapping pennants of
    joy.

I am the actor and the actress …. the voter .. the
    politician,
The emigrant and the exile .. the criminal that stood
    in the box,
He who has been famous, and he who shall be famous
    after today,
The stammerer …. the wellformed person .. the
    wasted or feeble person.

I am she who adorned herself and folded her hair
    expectantly,
My truant lover has come and it is dark.

Double yourself and receive me darkness,
Receive me and my lover too …. he will not let me go
    without him.

I roll myself upon you as upon a bed …. I resign
    myself to the dusk.
He whom I call answers me and takes the place of my
    lover,

He rises with me silently from the bed.

Darkness you are gentler than my lover .... his flesh
    was sweaty and panting,
I feel the hot moisture yet that he left me.

My hands are spread forth .. I pass them in all
    directions,
I would sound up the shadowy shore to which you are
    journeying.

Be careful, darkness .... already, what was it touched
    me?
I thought my lover had gone .... else darkness and he
    are one,
I hear the heart-beat .... I follow .. I fade away.

O hotcheeked and blushing! O foolish hectic!
O for pity's sake, no one must see me now! .... my
    clothes were stolen while I was abed,
Now I am thrust forth, where shall I run?

Pier that I saw dimly last night when I looked from
    the windows,
Pier out from the main, let me catch myself with you
    and stay .... I will not chafe you;
I feel ashamed to go naked about the world,

And am curious to know where my feet stand .... and
    what is this flooding me, childhood or manhood ....
    and the hunger that crosses the bridge between.

The cloth laps a first sweet eating and drinking,
Laps life-swelling yolks .... laps ear of rose-corn,
    milky and just ripened:
The white teeth stay, and the boss-tooth advances in
    darkness,
And liquor is spilled on lips and bosoms by touching
    glasses, and the best liquor afterward.

I descend my western course .... my sinews are
    flaccid,
Perfume and youth course through me, and I am their
    wake.

It is my face yellow and wrinkled instead of the old
    woman's,
I sit low in a strawbottom chair and carefully darn my
    grandson's stockings.

It is I too .... the sleepless widow looking out on the
    winter midnight,
I see the sparkles of starshine on the icy and pallid
    earth.

A shroud I see – and I am the shroud .... I wrap a
    body and lie in the coffin;
It is dark here underground .... it is not evil or pain
    here .... it is blank here, for reasons.

It seems to me that everything in the light and air
    ought to be happy;
Whoever is not in his coffin and the dark grave, let
    him know he has enough.

I see a beautiful gigantic swimmer swimming naked
    through the eddies of the sea,
His brown hair lies close and even to his head .... he
    strikes out with courageous arms .... he urges
    himself with his legs.

I see his white body .... I see his undaunted eyes;
I hate the swift-running eddies that would dash him
    headforemost on the rocks.

What are you doing you ruffianly red-trickled waves?
Will you kill the courageous giant? Will you kill him
    in the prime of his middle age?

Steady and long he struggles;
He is baffled and banged and bruised .... he holds out
    while his strength holds out,

The slapping eddies are spotted with his blood ....
    they bear him away .... they roll him and swing him
    and turn him:
His beautiful body is borne in the circling eddies .... it
    is continually bruised on rocks,
Swiftly and out of sight is borne the brave corpse.

I turn but do not extricate myself;
Confused .... a pastreading .... another, but with
    darkness yet.

The beach is cut by the razory ice-wind .... the
    wreck-guns sound,
The tempest lulls and the moon comes floundering
    through the drifts.

I look where the ship helplessly heads end on I
    hear the burst as she strikes .. I hear the howls of
    dismay .... they grow fainter and fainter.

I cannot aid with my wringing fingers;
I can but rush to the surf and let it drench me and
    freeze upon me.

I search with the crowd .... not one of the company is
    washed to us alive;

In the morning I help pick up the dead and lay them
    in rows in a barn.

Now of the old war-days .. the defeat at Brooklyn;
Washington stands inside the lines .. he stands on the
    entrenched hills amid a crowd of officers,
His face is cold and damp .... he cannot repress the
    weeping drops .... he lifts the glass perpetually to
    his eyes .... the color is blanched from his cheeks,
He sees the slaughter of the southern braves confided
    to him by their parents.

The same at last and at last when peace is declared,
He stands in the room of the old tavern .... the
    wellbeloved soldiers all pass through,
The officers speechless and slow draw near in their
    turns,
The chief encircles their necks with his arm and
    kisses them on the cheek,
He kisses lightly the wet cheeks one after another
    .... he shakes hands and bids goodbye to the army.

Now I tell what my mother told me today as we sat at
    dinner together,
Of when she was a nearly grown girl living home with
    her parents on the old homestead.

A red squaw came one breakfasttime to the old
    homestead,
On her back she carried a bundle of rushes for
    rushbottoming chairs;
Her hair straight shiny coarse black and profuse
    halfenveloped her face,
Her step was free and elastic .... her voice sounded
    exquisitely as she spoke.

My mother looked in delight and amazement at the
    stranger,
She looked at the beauty of her tallborne face and full
    and pliant limbs,
The more she looked upon her she loved her,
Never before had she seen such wonderful beauty and
    purity;
She made her sit on a bench by the jamb of the
    fireplace .... she cooked food for her,
She had no work to give her but she gave her
    remembrance and fondness.

The red squaw staid all the forenoon, and toward the
    middle of the afternoon she went away;
O my mother was loth to have her go away,
All the week she thought of her .... she watched for
    her many a month,

She remembered her many a winter and many a
    summer,
But the red squaw never came nor was heard of there
    again.

Now Lucifer was not dead .... or if he was I am his
    sorrowful terrible heir;
I have been wronged .... I am oppressed .... I hate
    him that oppresses me,
I will either destroy him, or he shall release me.

Damn him! how he does defile me,
How he informs against my brother and sister and
    takes pay for their blood,
How he laughs when I look down the bend after the
    steamboat that carries away my woman.

Now the vast dusk bulk that is the whale's bulk .... it
    seems mine,
Warily, sportsman! though I lie so sleepy and
    sluggish, my tap is death.

A show of the summer softness .... a contact of
    something unseen .... an amour of the light and air;
I am jealous and overwhelmed with friendliness,
And will go gallivant with the light and the air myself,

And have an unseen something to be in contact with
    them also.

O love and summer! you are in the dreams and in me,
Autumn and winter are in the dreams .... the farmer
    goes with his thrift,
The droves and crops increase .... the barns are
    wellfilled.

Elements merge in the night .... ships make tacks in
    the dreams .... the sailor sails .... the exile returns
    home,
The fugitive returns unharmed .... the immigrant is
    back beyond months and years;
The poor Irishman lives in the simple house of his
    childhood, with the wellknown neighbors and
    faces,
They warmly welcome him .... he is barefoot again
    .... he forgets he is welloff;
The Dutchman voyages home, and the Scotchman
    and Welchman voyage home .. and the native of the
    Mediterranean voyages home;
To every port of England and France and Spain enter
    wellfilled ships;
The Swiss foots it toward his hills .... the Prussian
    goes his way, and the Hungarian his way, and the
    Pole goes his way,

The Swede returns, and the Dane and Norwegian
    return.

The homeward bound and the outward bound,
The beautiful lost swimmer, the ennuyee, the onanist,
    the female that loves unrequited, the moneymaker,
The actor and actress .. those through with their parts
    and those waiting to commence,
The affectionate boy, the husband and wife, the
    voter, the nominee that is chosen and the nominee
    that has failed,
The great already known, and the great anytime after
    to day,
The stammerer, the sick, the perfectformed, the
    homely,
The criminal that stood in the box, the judge that sat
    and sentenced him, the fluent lawyers, the jury, the
    audience,
The laugher and weeper, the dancer, the midnight
    widow, the red squaw,
The consumptive, the erysipalite, the idiot, he that is
    wronged,
The antipodes, and every one between this and them
    in the dark,
I swear they are averaged now .... one is no better
    than the other,

The night and sleep have likened them and restored
  them.

I swear they are all beautiful,
Every one that sleeps is beautiful .... every thing in
  the dim night is beautiful,
The wildest and bloodiest is over and all is peace.

Peace is always beautiful,
The myth of heaven indicates peace and night.

The myth of heaven indicates the soul;
The soul is always beautiful .... it appears more or it
  appears less .... it comes or lags behind,
It comes from its embowered garden and looks
  pleasantly on itself and encloses the world;
Perfect and clean the genitals previously jetting, and
  perfect and clean the womb cohering,
The head wellgrown and proportioned and plumb,
  and the bowels and joints proportioned and plumb.

The soul is always beautiful,
The universe is duly in order .... every thing is in its
  place,
What is arrived is in its place, and what waits is in its
  place;

The twisted skull waits .... the watery or rotten blood
    waits,
The child of the glutton or venerealee waits long, and
    the child of the drunkard waits long, and the
    drunkard himself waits long,
The sleepers that lived and died wait .... the far
    advanced are to go on in their turns, and the far
    behind are to go on in their turns,
The diverse shall be no less diverse, but they shall
    flow and unite .... they unite now.

The sleepers are very beautiful as they lie unclothed,
They flow hand in hand over the whole earth from
    east to west as they lie un-clothed;
The Asiatic and African are hand in hand .... the
    European and American are hand in hand,
Learned and unlearned are hand in hand .. and male
    and female are hand in hand;
The bare arm of the girl crosses the bare breast of her
    lover .... they press close without lust .... his lips
    press her neck,
The father holds his grown or ungrown son in his
    arms with measureless love .... and the son holds
    the father in his arms with measureless love,
The white hair of the mother shines on the white
    wrist of the daughter,

The breath of the boy goes with the breath of the man
     .... friend is inarmed by friend,
The scholar kisses the teacher and the teacher kisses
     the scholar .... the wronged is made right,
The call of the slave is one with the master's call ..
     and the master salutes the slave,
The felon steps forth from the prison .... the insane
     becomes sane .... the suffering of sick persons is
     relieved,
The sweatings and fevers stop .. the throat that was
     unsound is sound .. the lungs of the consumptive
     are resumed .. the poor distressed head is free,
The joints of the rheumatic move as smoothly as ever,
     and smoother than ever,
Stiflings and passages open .... the paralysed become
     supple,
The swelled and convulsed and congested awake to
     themselves in condition,
They pass the invigoration of the night and the
     chemistry of the night and awake.

I too pass from the night;
I stay awhile away O night, but I return to you again
     and love you;
Why should I be afraid to trust myself to you?
I am not afraid .... I have been well brought forward
     by you;

I love the rich running day, but I do not desert her in
    whom I lay so long:
I know not how I came of you, and I know not where
    I go with you .... but I know I came well and shall
    go well.

I will stop only a time with the night .... and rise
    betimes.

I will duly pass the day O my mother and duly return
    to you;
Not you will yield forth the dawn again more surely
    than you will yield forth me again,
Not the womb yields the babe in its time more surely
    than I shall be yielded from you in my time.

I Sing the Body Electric

The bodies of men and women engirth me, and I
    engirth them,
They will not let me off nor I them till I go with them
    and respond to them and love them.

Was it dreamed whether those who corrupted their
    own live bodies could conceal themselves?
And whether those who defiled the living were as bad
    as they who defiled the dead?

The expression of the body of man or woman balks
    account,
The male is perfect and that of the female is perfect.

The expression of a wellmade man appears not only
    in his face,
It is in his limbs and joints also .... it is curiously in
    the joints of his hips and wrists,
It is in his walk .. the carriage of his neck .. the flex of
    his waist and knees .... dress does not hide him,
The strong sweet supple quality he has strikes
    through the cotton and flannel;
To see him pass conveys as much as the best poem ..
    perhaps more,

Originally untitled

You linger to see his back and the back of his neck
    and shoulderside.

The sprawl and fulness of babes .... the bosoms and
    heads of women .... the folds of their dress .... their
    style as we pass in the street .... the contour of their
    shape downwards;
The swimmer naked in the swimmingbath .. seen as
    he swims through the salt transparent greenshine,
    or lies on his back and rolls silently with the heave
    of the water;
Framers bare-armed framing a house .. hoisting the
    beams in their places .. or using the mallet and
    mortising-chisel,
The bending forward and backward of rowers in
    rowboats .... the horseman in his saddle;
Girls and mothers and housekeepers in all their
    exquisite offices,
The group of laborers seated at noontime with their
    open dinnerkettles, and their wives waiting,
The female soothing a child .... the farmer's daughter
    in the garden or cowyard,
The woodman rapidly swinging his axe in the woods
    .... the young fellow hoeing corn .... the
    sleighdriver guiding his six horses through the
    crowd,

The wrestle of wrestlers .. two apprentice-boys, quite
    grown, lusty, goodnatured, nativeborn, out on the
    vacant lot at sundown after work,
The coats vests and caps thrown down .. the embrace
    of love and resistance,
The upperhold and underhold – the hair rumpled
    over and blinding the eyes;
The march of firemen in their own costumes – the
    play of the masculine muscle through cleansetting
    trowsers and waistbands,
The slow return from the fire .... the pause when the
    bell strikes suddenly again – the listening on the
    alert,
The natural perfect and varied attitudes .... the bent
    head, the curved neck, the counting:
Suchlike I love .... I loosen myself and pass freely
    .... and am at the mother's breast with the little
    child,
And swim with the swimmer, and wrestle with
    wrestlers, and march in line with the firemen, and
    pause and listen and count.

I knew a man .... he was a common farmer .... he was
    the father of five sons ... and in them were the
    fathers of sons ... and in them were the fathers of
    sons.

This man was of wonderful vigor and calmness and
    beauty of person;
The shape of his head, the richness and breadth of his
    manners, the pale yellow and white of his hair and
    beard, the immeasurable meaning of his black eyes,
These I used to go and visit him to see .... He was
    wise also,
He was six feet tall .... he was over eighty years old
    .... his sons were massive clean bearded tanfaced
    and handsome,
They and his daughters loved him ... all who saw him
    loved him ... they did not love him by allowance ...
    they loved him with personal love;
He drank water only .... the blood showed like scarlet
    through the clear brown skin of his face;
He was a frequent gunner and fisher ... he sailed his
    boat himself ... he had a fine one presented to him
    by a shipjoiner .... he had fowling-pieces, presented
    to him by men that loved him;
When he went with his five sons and many grandsons
    to hunt or fish you would pick him out as the most
    beautiful and vigorous of the gang,
You would wish long and long to be with him .... you
    would wish to sit by him in the boat that you and
    he might touch each other.

I have perceived that to be with those I like is
    enough,
To stop in company with the rest at evening is
    enough,
To be surrounded by beautiful curious breathing
    laughing flesh is enough,
To pass among them .. to touch any one .... to rest
    my arm ever so lightly round his or her neck for a
    moment .... what is this then?
I do not ask any more delight .... I swim in it as in a
    sea.

There is something in staying close to men and
    women and looking on them and in the contact and
    odor of them that pleases the soul well,
All things please the soul, but these please the soul
    well.

This is the female form,
A divine nimbus exhales from it from head to foot,
It attracts with fierce undeniable attraction,
I am drawn by its breath as if I were no more than a
    helpless vapor .... all falls aside but myself and it,
Books, art, religion, time .. the visible and solid earth
    .. the atmosphere and the fringed clouds .. what
    was expected of heaven or feared of hell are now
    consumed,

Mad filaments, ungovernable shoots play out of it ..
    the response likewise ungovernable,
Hair, bosom, hips, bend of legs, negligent falling
    hands – all diffused .... mine too diffused,
Ebb stung by the flow, and flow stung by the ebb
    .... loveflesh swelling and deliciously aching,
Limitless limpid jets of love hot and enormous ....
    quivering jelly of love ... white-blow and delirious
    juice,
Bridegroom-night of love working surely and softly
    into the prostrate dawn,
Undulating into the willing and yielding day,
Lost in the cleave of the clasping and sweetfleshed
    day.

This is the nucleus ... after the child is born of woman
    the man is born of woman,
This is the bath of birth ... this is the merge of small
    and large and the outlet again.

Be not ashamed women .. your privilege encloses the
    rest .. it is the exit of the rest,
You are the gates of the body and you are the gates of
    the soul.

The female contains all qualities and tempers them
    .... she is in her place .... she moves with perfect
    balance,
She is all things duly veiled .... she is both passive and
    active .... she is to conceive daughters as well as
    sons and sons as well as daughters.

As I see my soul reflected in nature .... as I see
    through a mist one with inexpressible completeness
    and beauty .... see the bent head and arms folded
    over the breast .... the female I see,
I see the bearer of the great fruit which is immortality
    .... the good thereof is not tasted by roues, and
    never can be.

The male is not less the soul, nor more .... he too is in
    his place,
He too is all qualities .... he is action and power
    .... the flush of the known universe is in him,
Scorn becomes him well and appetite and defiance
    become him well,
The fiercest largest passions .. bliss that is utmost and
    sorrow that is utmost become him well .... pride is
    for him,
The fullspread pride of man is calming and excellent
    to the soul;

Knowledge becomes him .... he likes it always .... he
    brings everything to the test of himself,
Whatever the survey .. whatever the sea and the sail,
    he strikes soundings at last only here,
Where else does he strike soundings except here?

The man's body is sacred and the woman's body is
    sacred .... it is no matter who,
Is it a slave? Is it one of the dullfaced immigrants just
    landed on the wharf?

Each belongs here or anywhere just as much as the
    welloff .... just as much as you,
Each has his or her place in the procession.

All is a procession,
The universe is a procession with measured and
    beautiful motion.

Do you know so much that you call the slave or the
    dullface ignorant?
Do you suppose you have a right to a good sight ...
    and he or she has no right to a sight?
Do you think matter has cohered together from its
    diffused float, and the soil is on the surface and
    water runs and vegetation sprouts for you .. and not
    for him and her?

A slave at auction!
I help the auctioneer .... the sloven does not half
    know his business.

Gentlemen look on this curious creature,
Whatever the bids of the bidders they cannot be high
    enough for him,
For him the globe lay preparing quintillions of years
    without one animal or plant,
For him the revolving cycles truly and steadily rolled.

In that head the allbaffling brain,
In it and below it the making of the attributes of
    heroes.

Examine these limbs, red black or white .... they are
    very cunning in tendon and nerve;
They shall be stript that you may see them.

Exquisite senses, lifelit eyes, pluck, volition,
Flakes of breastmuscle, pliant backbone and neck,
    flesh not flabby, goodsized arms and legs,
And wonders within there yet.

Within there runs his blood .... the same old blood ..
    the same red running blood;

There swells and jets his heart .... There all passions
    and desires .. all reachings and aspirations:
Do you think they are not there because they are not
    expressed in parlors and lecture-rooms?

This is not only one man .... he is the father of those
    who shall be fathers in their turns,
In him the start of populous states and rich republics,
Of him countless immortal lives with countless
    embodiments and enjoyments.

How do you know who shall come from the offspring
    of his offspring through the centuries?
Who might you find you have come from yourself if
    you could trace back through the centuries?

A woman at auction,
She too is not only herself .... she is the teeming
    mother of mothers,
She is the bearer of them that shall grow and be mates
    to the mothers.

Her daughters or their daughters' daughters .. who
    knows who shall mate with them?
Who knows through the centuries what heroes may
    come from them?

In them and of them natal love .... in them the divine
  mystery .... the same old beautiful mystery.

Have you ever loved a woman?
Your mother .... is she living? .... Have you been
  much with her? and has she been much with you?
Do you not see that these are exactly the same to all
  in all nations and times all over the earth?

If life and the soul are sacred the human body is
  sacred;
And the glory and sweet of a man is the token of
  manhood untainted,
And in man or woman a clean strong firmfibred body
  is beautiful as the most beautiful face.

Have you seen the fool that corrupted his own live
  body? or the fool that corrupted her own live body?
For they do not conceal themselves, and cannot
  conceal themselves.

Who degrades or defiles the living human body is
  cursed,
Who degrades or defiles the body of the dead is not
  more cursed.

Crossing Brooklyn Ferry

Flood-tide of the river, flow on! I watch you, face to
    face,
Clouds of the west! sun half an hour high! I see you
    also face to face.

Crowds of men and women attired in the usual
    costumes, how curious you are to me!
On the ferry-boats the hundreds and hundreds that
    cross are more curious to me than you suppose,
And you that shall cross from shore to shore years
    hence, are more to me, and more in my
    meditations, than you might suppose.

The impalpable sustenance of me from all things at all
    hours of the day,
The simple, compact, well-joined scheme – myself
    disintegrated, every one disintegrated, yet part of
    the scheme,
The similitudes of the past and those of the future,
The glories strung like beads on my smallest sights
    and hearings – on the walk in the street, and the
    passage over the river,
The current rushing so swiftly, and swimming with
    me far away,

Original title: "Sun-Down Poem"

The others that are to follow me, the ties between me
    and them,
The certainty of others – the life, love, sight, hearing
    of others.

Others will enter the gates of the ferry, and cross
    from shore to shore,
Others will watch the run of the flood-tide,
Others will see the shipping of Manhattan north and
    west, and the heights of Brooklyn to the south and
    east,
Others will see the islands large and small,
Fifty years hence others will see them as they cross,
    the sun half an hour high,
A hundred years hence, or ever so many hundred
    years hence, others will see them,
Will enjoy the sun-set, the pouring in of the
    flood-tide, the falling back to the sea of the
    ebb-tide.

It avails not, neither time or place – distance avails
    not,
I am with you, you men and women of a generation,
    or ever so many generations hence,
I project myself, also I return – I am with you, and
    know how it is.

Just as you feel when you look on the river and sky,
   so I felt,
Just as any of you is one of a living crowd, I was one
   of a crowd,
Just as you are refreshed by the gladness of the river,
   and the bright flow, I was refreshed,
Just as you stand and lean on the rail, yet hurry with
   the swift current, I stood, yet was hurried,
Just as you look on the numberless masts of ships, and
   the thick-stemmed pipes of steamboats, I looked.

I too many and many a time crossed the river, the sun
   half an hour high,
I watched the December sea-gulls, I saw them high in
   the air floating with motionless wings oscillating
   their bodies,
I saw how the glistening yellow lit up parts of their
   bodies, and left the rest in strong shadow,
I saw the slow-wheeling circles and the gradual
   edging toward the south.

I too saw the reflection of the summer-sky in the
   water.
Had my eyes dazzled by the shimmering track of
   beams,
Looked at the fine centrifugal spokes of light round
   the shape of my head in the sun-lit water,

Looked on the haze on the hills southward and
  southwestward,
Looked on the vapor as it flew in fleeces tinged with
  violet,
Looked toward the lower bay to notice the arriving
  ships,
Saw their approach, saw aboard those that were near
  me,
Saw the white sails of schooners and sloops, saw the
  ships at anchor,
The sailors at work in the rigging or out astride the
  spars,
The round masts, the swinging motion of the hulls,
  the slender serpentine pennants,
The large and small steamers in motion, the pilots in
  their pilot-houses,
The white wake left by the passage, the quick
  tremulous whirl of the wheels,
The flags of all nations, the falling of them at sun-set,
The scallop-edged waves in the twilight, the ladled
  cups, the frolicsome crests and glistening,
The stretch afar growing dimmer and dimmer, the
  gray walls of the granite store-houses by the docks,
On the river the shadowy group, the big steam-tug
  closely flanked on each side by the barges – the
  hay-boat, the belated lighter,

On the neighboring shore the fires from the foundry
  chimneys burning high and glaringly into the night,
Casting their flicker of black, contrasted with wild
  red and yellow light, over the tops of houses, and
  down into the clefts of streets.

These and all else were to me the same as they are to
  you,
I project myself a moment to tell you – also I return.

I loved well those cities,
I loved well the stately and rapid river,
The men and women I saw were all near to me,
Others the same – others who look back on me,
  because I looked forward to them,
The time will come, though I stop here today and
  tonight.

What is it, then, between us? What is the count of the
  scores or hundreds of years between us?
Whatever it is, it avails not – distance avails not, and
  place avails not.

I too lived,
I too walked the streets of Manhattan Island, and
  bathed in the waters around it;

I too felt the curious abrupt questionings stir within
    me,
In the day, among crowds of people, sometimes they
    came upon me,
In my walks home late at night, or as I lay in my bed,
    they came upon me.

I too had been struck from the float forever held in
    solution,
I too had received identity by my body,
That I was, I knew was of my body, and what I
    should be, I knew I should be of my body.

It is not upon you alone the dark patches fall,
The dark threw patches down upon me also,
The best I had done seemed to me blank and
    suspicious,
My great thoughts, as I supposed them, were they not
    in reality meagre? Would not people laugh at me?

It is not you alone who know what it is to be evil,
I am he who knew what it was to be evil,
I too knitted the old knot of contrariety,
Blabbed, blushed, resented, lied, stole, grudged,
Had guile, anger, lust, hot wishes I dared not speak,
Was wayward, vain, greedy, shallow, sly, a solitary
    committer, a coward, a malignant person,

The wolf, the snake, the hog, not wanting in me,
The cheating look, the frivolous word, the adulterous
    wish, not wanting,
Refusals, hates, postponements, meanness, laziness,
    none of these wanting.

But I was a Manhattanese, free, friendly, and proud!
I was called by my nighest name by clear loud voices
    of young men as they saw me approaching or
    passing,
Felt their arms on my neck as I stood, or the
    negligent leaning of their flesh against me as I sat,
Saw many I loved in the street, or ferry-boat, or
    public assembly, yet never told them a word,
Lived the same life with the rest, the same old
    laughing, gnawing, sleeping,
Played the part that still looks back on the actor or
    actress,
The same old role, the role that is what we make it, as
    great as we like, or as small as we like, or both great
    and small.

Closer yet I approach you,
What thought you have of me, I had as much of you –
    I laid in my stores in advance,
I considered long and seriously of you before you
    were born.

Who was to know what should come home to me?
Who knows but I am enjoying this?
Who knows but I am as good as looking at you now,
    for all you cannot see me?

It is not you alone, nor I alone,
Not a few races, not a few generations, not a few
    centuries,
It is that each came, or comes, or shall come, from its
    due emission, without fail, either now, or then, or
    henceforth.

Every thing indicates – the smallest does, and the
    largest does,
A necessary film envelops all, and envelops the soul
    for a proper time.

Now I am curious what sight can ever be more stately
    and admirable to me than my masthemm'd
    Manhatta, my river and sun-set, and my
    scallop-edged waves of flood-tide, the sea-gulls
    oscillating their bodies, the hay-boat in the
    twilight, and the belated lighter,
Curious what gods can exceed these that clasp me by
    the hand, and with voices I love call me promptly
    and loudly by my nighest name as I approach,

Curious what is more subtle than this which ties me
    to the woman or man that looks in my face,
Which fuses me into you now, and pours my meaning
    into you.

We understand, then, do we not?
What I promised without mentioning it, have you not
    accepted?
What the study could not teach – what the preaching
    could not accomplish is accomplished, is it not?
What the push of reading could not start is started by
    me personally, is it not?

Flow on, river! Flow with the flood-tide, and ebb
    with the ebb-tide!
Frolic on, crested and scallop-edged waves!
Gorgeous clouds of the sun-set, drench with your
    splendor me, or the men and women generations
    after me!
Cross from shore to shore, countless crowds of
    passengers!
Stand up, tall masts of Manahatta! – stand up,
    beautiful hills of Brooklyn!
Bully for you! you proud, friendly, free
    Manhattanese!
Throb, baffled and curious brain! throw out questions
    and answers!

Suspend here and everywhere, eternal float of
   solution!
Blab, blush, lie, steal, you or I or any one after us!
Gaze, loving and thirsting eyes, in the house or street
   or public assembly!
Sound out, voices of young men! loudly and musically
   call me by my nighest name!
Live, old life! play the part that looks back on the
   actor or actress!
Play the old role, the role that is great or small,
   according as one makes it!
Consider, you who peruse me, whether I may not in
   unknown ways be looking upon you!
Be firm, rail over the river, to support those who lean
   idly, yet haste with the hasting current!
Fly on, sea-birds! fly sideways, or wheel in large
   circles high in the air!
Receive the summer-sky, you water! faithfully hold it
   till all downcast eyes have time to take it from you!
Diverge, fine spokes of light, from the shape of my
   head, or any one's head, in the sun-lit water!
Come on, ships, from the lower bay! pass up or down,
   white-sailed schooners, sloops, lighters!
Flaunt away, flags of all nations! be duly lowered at
   sun-set!

Burn high your fires, foundry chimneys! cast black
  shadows at night-fall! cast red and yellow light over
  the tops of the houses!
Appearances, now or henceforth, indicate what you
  are!
You necessary film, continue to envelop the soul!
About my body for me, and your body for you, be
  hung our divinest aromas!
Thrive, cities! Bring your freight, bring your shows,
  ample and sufficient rivers!
Expand, being than which none else is perhaps more
  spiritual!
Keep your places, objects than which none else is
  more lasting!

We descend upon you and all things, we arrest you
  all,
We realize the soul only by you, you faithful solids
  and fluids,
Through you color, form, location, sublimity,
  ideality,
Through you every proof, comparison, and all the
  suggestions and determinations of ourselves.

You have waited, you always wait, you dumb
  beautiful ministers! you novices!

We receive you with free sense at last, and are
  insatiate henceforward,
Not you any more shall be able to foil us, or withhold
  yourselves from us,
We use you, and do not cast you aside – we plant you
  permanently within us,
We fathom you not – we love you – there is
  perfection in you also,
You furnish your parts toward eternity,
Great or small, you furnish your parts toward the
  soul.

Song of the Open Road

Afoot and light-hearted I take to the open road!
Healthy, free, the world before me!
The long brown path before me, leading wherever I
    choose!

Henceforth I ask not good-fortune, I am
    good-fortune,
Henceforth I whimper no more, postpone no more,
    need nothing,
Strong and content, I travel the open road.

The earth – that is sufficient,
I do not want the constellations any nearer,
I know they are very well where they are,
I know they suffice for those who belong to them.

Still here I carry my old delicious burdens,
I carry them, men and women – I carry them with me
    wherever I go,
I swear it is impossible for me to get rid of them,
I am filled with them, and I will fill them in return.

You road I travel and look around! I believe you are
    not all that is here!

Original title: "Poem of The Road"

I believe that something unseen is also here.

Here is the profound lesson of reception, neither
    preference or denial,
The black with his woolly head, the felon, the
    diseased, the illiterate person, are not denied,
The birth, the hasting after the physician, the
    beggar's tramp, the drunkard's stagger, the
    laughing party of mechanics,
The escaped youth, the rich person's carriage, the
    fop, the eloping couple,
The early market-man, the hearse, the moving of
    furniture into the town, the return back from the
    town,
They pass, I also pass, any thing passes, none can be
    interdicted,
None but are accepted, none but are dear to me.

You air that serves me with breath to speak!
You objects that call from diffusion my meanings and
    give them shape!
You light that wraps me and all things in delicate
    equable showers!
You animals moving serenely over the earth!
You birds that wing yourselves through the air! you
    insects!

You sprouting growths from the farmers' fields! you
    stalks and weeds by the fences!
You paths worn in the irregular hollows by the
    road-sides!
I think you are latent with curious existences – you
    are so dear to me.

You flagged walks of the cities! you strong curbs at
    the edges!
You ferries! you planks and posts of wharves! you
        timber-lined sides! you distant ships!
You rows of houses! you window-pierced facades!
    you roofs!
You porches and entrances! you copings and iron
    guards!
You windows whose transparent shells might expose
    so much!
You doors and ascending steps! you arches!
You gray stones of interminable pavements! you
    trodden crossings!
From all that has been near you I believe you have
    imparted to yourselves, and now would impart the
    same secretly to me,
From the living and the dead I think you have
    peopled your impassive surfaces, and the spirits
    thereof would be evident and amicable with me.

The earth expanding right hand and left hand,
The picture alive, every part in its best light,
The music falling in where it is wanted, and stopping
    where it is not wanted,
The cheerful voice of the public road – the gay fresh
    sentiment of the road.

O highway I travel! O public road! do you say to me,
    Do not leave me?
Do you say, Venture not? If you leave me, you are
    lost?
Do you say, I am already prepared – I am well-beaten
    and undenied – Adhere to me?

O public road! I say back, I am not afraid to leave you
    – yet I love you,
You express me better than I can express myself,
You shall be more to me than my poem.

I think heroic deeds were all conceived in the open
    air,
I think I could stop here myself, and do miracles,
I think whatever I meet on the road I shall like, and
    whatever beholds me shall like me,
I think whoever I see must be happy.

From this hour, freedom!

From this hour, I ordain myself loosed of limits and
    imaginary lines!
Going where I list – my own master, total and
    absolute,
Listening to others, and considering well what they
    say,
Pausing, searching, receiving, contemplating,
Gently but with undeniable will divesting myself of
    the holds that would hold me.

I inhale great draughts of air,
The east and the west are mine, and the north and the
    south are mine.

I am larger than I thought!
I did not know I held so much goodness!

All seems beautiful to me,
I can repeat over to men and women, You have done
    such good to me, I would do the same to you.

I will recruit for myself and you as I go,
I will scatter myself among men and women as I go,
I will toss the new gladness and roughness among
    them;
Whoever denies me, it shall not trouble me,

Whoever accepts me, he or she shall be blessed, and
    shall bless me.

Now if a thousand perfect men were to appear, it
    would not amaze me,
Now if a thousand beautiful forms of women
    appeared, it would not astonish me.
Now I see the secret of the making of the best
    persons,
It is to grow in the open air, and to eat and sleep with
    the earth.

Here is space – here a great personal deed has room,
A great deed seizes upon the hearts of the whole race
    of men,
Its effusion of strength and will overwhelms law, and
    mocks all authority and all argument against it.

Here is the test of wisdom,
Wisdom is not finally tested in schools,
Wisdom cannot be passed from one having it, to
    another not having it,
Wisdom is of the soul, is not susceptible of proof, is
    its own proof,
Applies to all stages and objects and qualities, and is
    content,

Is the certainty of the reality and immortality of
     things, and the excellence of things,
Something there is in the float of the sight of things
     that provokes it out of the soul.

Now I re-examine philosophies and religions,
They may prove well in lecture-rooms, yet not prove
     at all under the spacious clouds, and along the
     landscape and flowing currents.

Here is realization,
Here is a man tallied – he realizes here what he has in
     him,
The animals, the past, the future, light, space,
     majesty, love, if they are vacant of you, you are
     vacant of them.

Only the kernel of every object nourishes;
Where is he who tears off the husks for you and me?
Where is he that undoes stratagems and envelopes for
     you and me?

Here is adhesiveness – it is not previously fashioned,
     it is apropos;
Do you know what it is as you pass to be loved by
     strangers?
Do you know the talk of those turning eye-balls?

Here is the efflux of the soul,
The efflux of the soul comes through beautiful gates
  of laws, provoking questions,
These yearnings, why are they? these thoughts in the
  darkness, why are they?
Why are there men and women that while they are
  nigh me the sun-light expands my blood?
Why when they leave me do my pennants of joy sink
  flat and lank?
Why are there trees I never walk under but large and
  melodious thoughts descend upon me?
(I think they hang there winter and summer on those
  trees, and always drop fruit as I pass;)
What is it I interchange so suddenly with strangers?
What with some driver as I ride on the seat by his
  side?
What with some fisherman, drawing his seine by the
  shore, as I walk by and pause?
What gives me to be free to a woman's or man's
  good-will? What gives them to be free to mine?

The efflux of the soul is happiness – here is
  happiness,
I think it pervades the air, waiting at all times,
Now it flows into us – we are rightly charged.

Here rises the fluid and attaching character;
The fluid and attaching character is the freshness and
    sweetness of man and woman,
The herbs of the morning sprout no fresher and
    sweeter every day out of the roots of themselves,
    than it sprouts fresh and sweet continually out of
    itself.

Toward the fluid and attaching character exudes the
    sweat of the love of young and old,
From it falls distilled the charm that mocks beauty
    and attainments,
Toward it heaves the shuddering longing ache of
    contact.

Allons! Whoever you are, come travel with me!
Traveling with me, you find what never tires.

The earth never tires!
The earth is rude, silent, incomprehensible at first –
    nature is rude and incomprehensible at first,
Be not discouraged – keep on – there are divine
    things, well enveloped,
I swear to you there are divine things more beautiful
    than words can tell!

Allons! We must not stop here!

However sweet these laid-up stores, however
  convenient this dwelling, we cannot remain here!
However sheltered this port, however calm these
  waters, we must not anchor here!
However welcome the hospitality that surrounds us,
  we are permitted to receive it but a little while.

Allons! the inducements shall be great to you,
We will sail pathless and wild seas,
We will go where winds blow, waves dash, and the
  Yankee clipper speeds by under full sail.

Allons! With power, liberty, the earth, the elements!
Health, defiance, gaiety, self-esteem, curiosity!

Allons! From all formulas!
From your formulas, O bat-eyed and materialistic
  priests!

The stale cadaver blocks up the passage – the burial
  waits no longer.

Allons! Yet take warning!
He traveling with me needs the best blood, thews,
  endurance,
None may come to the trial till he or she bring
  courage and health.

Come not here if you have already spent the best of
  yourself!
Only those may come who come in sweet and
  determined bodies,
No diseased person – no rum-drinker or venereal
  taint is permitted here.

I and mine do not convince by arguments, similes,
  rhymes,
We convince by our presence.

Listen! I will be honest with you,
I do not offer the old smooth prizes, but offer rough
  new prizes,
These are the days that must happen to you:
You shall not heap up what is called riches,
You shall scatter with lavish hand all that you earn or
  achieve,
You but arrive at the city to which you were destined
  – you hardly settle yourself to satisfaction, before
  you are called by an irresistible call to depart,
You shall be treated to the ironical smiles and
  mockings of those who remain behind you,
What beckonings of love you receive, you shall only
  answer with passionate kisses of parting,

You shall not allow the hold of those who spread their
   reached hands toward you.

Allons! After the great companions! and to belong to
   them!
They too are on the road! they are the swift and
   majestic men! they are the greatest women!

Over that which hindered them, over that which
   retarded, passing impediments large or small,
Committers of crimes, committers of many beautiful
   virtues,
Enjoyers of calms of seas, and storms of seas,
Sailors of many a ship, walkers of many a mile of
   land,
Habitues of many different countries, habitues of
   far-distant dwellings,
Trusters of men and women, observers of cities,
   solitary toilers,
Pausers and contemplaters of tufts, blossoms, shells of
   the shore,
Dancers at wedding-dances, kissers of brides, tender
   helpers of children, bearers of children,
Soldiers of revolts, standers by gaping graves,
   lowerers down of coffins,

Journeyers over consecutive seasons, over the years –
    the curious years, each emerging from that which
    preceded it,
Journeyers as with companions, namely, their own
    diverse phases,
Forth-steppers from the latent unrealized baby-days,
Journeyers gaily with their own youth – journeyers
    with their bearded and well-grained manhood,
Journeyers with their womanhood, ample,
    unsurpassed, content,
Journeyers with their sublime old age of manhood or
    womanhood,
Old age, calm, expanded, broad with the haughty
    breadth of the universe,
Old age, flowing free with the delicious near-by
    freedom of death.

Allons! to that which is endless as it was
    beginningless!
To undergo much, tramps of days, rests of nights!
To merge all in the travel they tend to, and the days
    and nights they tend to!
Again to merge them in the start of superior journeys!
To see nothing anywhere but what you may reach it
    and pass it!
To conceive no time, however distant, but what you
    may reach it and pass it!

To look up or down no road but it stretches and waits
    for you! however long, but it stretches and waits for
    you!
To see no being, not God's or any, but you also go
    thither!
To see no possession but you may possess it! enjoying
    all without labor or purchase – abstracting the feast,
    yet not abstracting one particle of it;
To take the best of the farmer's farm and the rich
    man's elegant villa, and the chaste blessings of the
    well-married couple, and the fruits of orchards and
    flowers of gardens!
To take to your use out of the compact cities as you
    pass through!
To carry buildings and streets with you afterward
    wherever you go!
To gather the minds of men out of their brains as you
    encounter them! to gather the love out of their
    hearts!
To take your own lovers on the road with you, for all
    that you leave them behind you!
To know the universe itself as a road – as many roads
    – as roads for traveling souls!

The soul travels,
The body does not travel as much as the soul,

The body has just as great a work as the soul, and
  parts away at last for the journeys of the soul.

All parts away for the progress of souls,
All religion, all solid things, arts, governments – all
  that was or is apparent upon this globe or any
  globe, falls into niches and corners before the
  processions of souls along the grand roads of the
  universe,
Of the progress of the souls of men and women along
  the grand roads of the universe, all other progress is
  the needed emblem and sustenance.

Forever alive, forever forward,
Stately, solemn, sad, withdrawn, baffled, mad,
  turbulent, feeble, dissatisfied,
Desperate, proud, fond, sick, accepted by men,
  rejected by men,
They go! they go! I know that they go, but I know
  not where they go,
But I know that they go toward the best – toward
  something great.

Allons! Whoever you are! come forth!
You must not stay in your house, though you built it,
  or though it has been built for you.

Allons! out of the dark confinement!
It is useless to protest – I know all, and expose it.

Behold through you as bad as the rest!
Through the laughter, dancing, dining, supping, of
    people,
Inside of dresses and ornaments, inside of those
    washed and trimmed faces,
Behold a secret silent loathing and despair!

No husband, no wife, no friend, no lover, so trusted
    as to hear the confession,
Another self, a duplicate of every one, skulking and
    hiding it goes, open and above-board it goes,
Formless and wordless through the streets of the
    cities, polite and bland in the parlors,
In the cars of rail-roads, in steam-boats, in the public
    assembly,
Home to the houses of men and women, among their
    families, at the table, in the bed-room, everywhere,
Smartly attired, countenance smiling, form upright,
    death under the breast-bones, hell under the
    skull-bones,
Under the broad-cloth and gloves, under the ribbons
    and artificial flowers,
Keeping fair with the customs, speaking not a syllable
    of itself,

Speaking of anything else, but never of itself.

Allons! through struggles and wars!
The goal that was named cannot be countermanded.

Have the past struggles succeeded?
What has succeeded? Yourself? Your nation? Nature?
Now understand me well – it is provided in the
    essence of things, that from any fruition of success,
    no matter what, shall come forth something to
    make a greater struggle necessary.

My call is the call of battle – I nourish active
    rebellion,
He going with me must go well armed,
He going with me goes often with spare diet, poverty,
    angry enemies, contentions.

Allons! the road is before us!
It is safe – I have tried it – my own feet have tried it
    well.

Allons! be not detained!
Let the paper remain on the desk unwritten, and the
    book on the shelf unopened!
Let the tools remain in the work-shop! let the money
    remain unearned!

Let the school stand! mind not the cry of the teacher!
Let the preacher preach in his pulpit! let the lawyer
    plead in the court, and the judge expound the law!

Mon enfant! I give you my hand!
I give you my love, more precious than money,
I give you myself, before preaching or law;
Will you give me yourself? Will you come travel with
    me?
Shall we stick by each other as long as we live?

A Song of the Rolling Earth

Earth, round, rolling, compact – suns, moons,
    animals – all these are words,
Watery, vegetable, sauroid advances – beings,
    premonitions, lispings of the future – these are vast
    words.

Were you thinking that those were the words – those
    upright lines? those curves, angles, dots?
No, those are not the words – the substantial words
    are in the ground and sea,
They are in the air – they are in you.

Were you thinking that those were the words – those
    delicious sounds out of your friends' mouths?
No, the real words are more delicious than they.

Human bodies are words, myriads of words,
In the best poems re-appears the body, man's or
    woman's, well-shaped, natural, gay,
Every part able, active, receptive, without shame or
    the need of shame.

Air, soil, water, fire, these are words,

Original title: "Poem of the Sayers of The Words of The Earth"

I myself am a word with them – my qualities
    interpenetrate with theirs – my name is nothing to
    them,
Though it were told in the three thousand languages,
    what would air, soil, water, fire, know of my name?

A healthy presence, a friendly or commanding
    gesture, are words, sayings, meanings,
The charms that go with the mere looks of some men
    and women are sayings and meanings also.

The workmanship of souls is by the inaudible words
    of the earth,
The great masters, the sayers, know the earth's
    words, and use them more than the audible words.

Syllables are not the earth's words,
Beauty, reality, manhood, time, life – the realities of
    such as these are the earth's words.

Amelioration is one of the earth's words,
The earth neither lags nor hastens,
It has all attributes, growths, effects, latent in itself
    from the jump,
It is not half beautiful only   defects and excrescences
    show just as much as perfections show.

The earth does not withhold, it is generous enough,
The truths of the earth continually wait, they are not
    so concealed either,
They are calm, subtle, untransmissible by print,
They are imbued through all things, conveying
    themselves willingly,
Conveying a sentiment and invitation of the earth – I
    utter and utter,
I speak not, yet if you hear me not, of what avail am I
    to you?
To bear – to better – lacking these, of what avail am
    I?

Accouche! Accouchez!
Will you rot your own fruit in yourself there?
Will you squat and stifle there?

The earth does not argue,
Is not pathetic, has no arrangements,
Does not scream, haste, persuade, threaten, promise,
Makes no discriminations, has no conceivable
    failures,
Closes nothing, refuses nothing, shuts none out,
Of all the powers, objects, states, it notifies, shuts
    none out.

The earth does not exhibit itself nor refuse to exhibit
    itself – possesses still underneath,
Underneath the ostensible sounds, the august chorus
    of heroes, the wail of slaves,
Persuasions of lovers, curses, gasps of the dying,
    laughter of young people, accents of bargainers,
Underneath these possessing the words that never
    fail.

To her children the words of the eloquent dumb great
    mother never fail,
The true words do not fail, for motion does not fail,
    and reflection does not fail,
Also the day and night do not fail, and the voyage we
    pursue does not fail.

Of the interminable sisters,
Of the ceaseless cotillions of sisters,
Of the centripetal and centrifugal sisters, the elder
    and younger sisters,
The beautiful sister we know dances on with the rest.

With her ample back toward every beholder,
With the fascinations of youth and the equal
    fascinations of age,
Sits she whom I too love like the rest, sits
    undisturbed,

Holding up in her hand what has the character of a
  mirror, her eyes glancing back from it,
Glancing thence as she sits, inviting none, denying
  none,
Holding a mirror day and night tirelessly before her
  own face.

Seen at hand, or seen at a distance,
Duly the twenty-four appear in public every day,
Duly approach and pass with their companions, or a
  companion,
Looking from no countenances of their own, but from
  the countenances of those who are with them,
From the countenances of children or women, or the
  manly countenance,
From the open countenances of animals, from
  inanimate things,
From the landscape or waters, or from the exquisite
  apparition of the sky,
From our own countenances, mine and yours,
  faithfully returning them,
Every day in public appearing without fail, but never
  twice with the same companions.

Embracing man, embracing all, proceed the three
  hundred and sixty-five resistlessly round the sun,

Embracing all, soothing, supporting, follow close
    three hundred and sixty-five offsets of the first,
    sure and necessary as they.

Tumbling on steadily, nothing dreading,
Sunshine, storm, cold, heat, forever withstanding,
    passing, carrying,
The soul's realization and determination still
    inheriting,
The liquid vacuum around and ahead still entering
    and dividing,
No balk retarding, no anchor anchoring, on no rock
    striking,
Swift, glad, content, unbereaved, nothing losing,
Of all able and ready at any time to give strict
    account,
The divine ship sails the divine sea.

Whoever you are! motion and reflection are especially
    for you,
The divine ship sails the divine sea for you.

Whoever you are! you are he or she for whom the
    earth is solid and liquid,
You are he or she for whom the sun and moon hang
    in the sky,
For none more than you are the present and the past,

For none more than you is immortality.

Each man to himself, and each woman to herself, is
    the word of the past and present, and the word of
    immortality,
Not one can acquire for another – not one!
Not one can grow for another – not one!

The song is to the singer, and comes back most to
    him,
The teaching is to the teacher, and comes back most
    to him,
The murder is to the murderer, and comes back most
    to him,
The theft is to the thief, and comes back most to him,
The love is to the lover, and comes back most to him,
The gift is to the giver, and comes back most to him –
    it cannot fail,
The oration is to the orator, and the acting is to the
    actor and actress, not to the audience,
And no man understands any greatness or goodness
    but his own, or the indication of his own.

I swear the earth shall surely be complete to him or
    her who shall be complete!
I swear the earth remains broken and jagged only to
    him or her who remains broken and jagged!

I swear there is no greatness or power that does not
    emulate those of the earth!
I swear there can be no theory of any account, unless
    it corroborate the theory of the earth!
No politics, art, religion, behaviour, or what not, is of
    account, unless it compare with the amplitude of
    the earth,
Unless it face the exactness, vitality, impartiality,
    rectitude of the earth.

I swear I begin to see love with sweeter spasms than
    that which responds love!
It is that which contains itself, which never invites
    and never refuses.

I swear I begin to see little or nothing in audible
    words!
I swear I think all merges toward the presentation of
    the unspoken meanings of the earth!
Toward him who sings the songs of the body, and of
    the truths of the earth,
Toward him who makes the dictionaries of the words
    that print cannot touch.

I swear I see what is better than to tell the best,
It is always to leave the best untold.

When I undertake to tell the best, I find I cannot,
My tongue is ineffectual on its pivots,
My breath will not be obedient to its organs,
I become a dumb man.

The best of the earth cannot be told anyhow – all or
   any is best,
It is not what you anticipated, it is cheaper, easier,
   nearer,
Things are not dismissed from the places they held
   before,
The earth is just as positive and direct as it was
   before,
Facts, religions, improvements, politics, trades, are as
   real as before,
But the soul is also real, it too is positive and direct,
No reasoning, no proof has established it,
Undeniable growth has established it.

This is a poem for the sayers of the earth – these are
   hints of meanings,
These are they that echo the tones of souls, and the
   phrases of souls;
If they did not echo the phrases of souls, what were
   they then?

If they had not reference to you in especial, what
  were they then?

I swear I will never henceforth have to do with the
  faith that tells the best!
I will have to do with that faith only that leaves the
  best untold.

Say on, sayers of the earth!
Delve! mould! pile the substantial words of the earth!
Work on, age after age! nothing is to be lost,
It may have to wait long, but it will certainly come in
  use,
When the materials are all prepared, the architects
  shall appear,
I swear to you the architects shall appear without fail!
  I announce them and lead them!
I swear to you they will understand you and justify
  you!
I swear to you the greatest among them shall be he
  who best knows you, and encloses all, and is
  faithful to all!
I swear to you, he and the rest shall not forget you!
  they shall perceive that you are not an iota less than
  they!
I swear to you, you shall be glorified in them!

As I Ebb'd with the Ocean of Life

Elemental drifts!
O I wish I could impress others as you and the waves
  have just been impressing me.

As I ebbed with an ebb of the ocean of life,
As I wended the shores I know,
As I walked where the sea-ripples wash you,
  Paumanok,
Where they rustle up, hoarse and sibilant,
Where the fierce old mother endlessly cries for her
  castaways,
I, musing, late in the autumn day, gazing off
  southward,
Alone, held by the eternal self of me that threatens to
  get the better of me, and stifle me,
Was seized by the spirit that trails in the lines
  underfoot,
In the rim, the sediment, that stands for all the water
  and all the land of the globe.

Fascinated, my eyes, reverting from the south,
  dropped, to follow those slender winrows,
Chaff, straw, splinters of wood, weeds, and the
  sea-gluten,

Originally #1 in the *Leaves of Grass* cluster

Scum, scales from shining rocks, leaves of
    salt-lettuce, left by the tide;
Miles walking, the sound of breaking waves the other
    side of me,
Paumanok, there and then, as I thought the old
    thought of likenesses,
These you presented to me, you fish-shaped island,
As I wended the shores I know,
As I walked with that eternal self of me, seeking
    types.

As I wend the shores I know not,
As I listen to the dirge, the voices of men and women
    wrecked,
As I inhale the impalpable breezes that set in upon
    me,
As the ocean so mysterious rolls toward me closer and
    closer,
At once I find, the least thing that belongs to me, or
    that I see or touch, I know not;
I, too, but signify, at the utmost, a little washed-up
    drift,
A few sands and dead leaves to gather,
Gather, and merge myself as part of the sands and
    drift.

O baffled, balked,

Bent to the very earth, here preceding what follows,
Oppressed with myself that I have dared to open my
     mouth,
Aware now, that, amid all the blab whose echoes
     recoil upon me, I have not once had the least idea
     who or what I am,
But that before all my insolent poems the real ME
     still stands untouched, untold, altogether
     unreached,
Withdrawn far, mocking me with
     mock-congratulatory signs and bows,
With peals of distant ironical laughter at every word
I have written or shall write,
Striking me with insults till I fall helpless upon the
     sand.

O I perceive I have not understood anything – not a
     single object – and that no man ever can.

I perceive Nature here, in sight of the sea, is taking
     advantage of me, to dart upon me, and sting me,
Because I was assuming so much,
And because I have dared to open my mouth to sing
     at all.

You oceans both! You tangible land! Nature!

Be not too rough with me – I submit – I close with
    you,
These little shreds shall, indeed, stand for all.

You friable shore, with trails of debris!
You fish-shaped island! I take what is underfoot;
What is yours is mine, my father.

I too Paumanok,
I too have bubbled up, floated the measureless float,
    and been washed on your shores;
I too am but a trail of drift and debris,
I too leave little wrecks upon you, you fish-shaped
    island.

I throw myself upon your breast, my father,
I cling to you so that you cannot unloose me,
I hold you so firm, till you answer me something.

Kiss me, my father,
Touch me with your lips, as I touch those I love,
Breathe to me, while I hold you close, the secret of
    the wondrous murmuring I envy,
For I fear I shall become crazed, if I cannot emulate
    it, and utter myself as well as it.

Sea-raff! Crook-tongued waves!

O, I will yet sing, some day, what you have said to
    me.

Ebb, ocean of life, (the flow will return,)
Cease not your moaning, you fierce old mother,
Endlessly cry for your castaways – but fear not, deny
    not me,
Rustle not up so hoarse and angry against my feet, as
    I touch you, or gather from you.

I mean tenderly by you,
I gather for myself, and for this phantom, looking
    down where we lead, and following me and mine.

Me and mine!
We, loose winrows, little corpses,
Froth, snowy white, and bubbles,
(See! from my dead lips the ooze exuding at last!
See – the prismatic colors, glistening and rolling!)
Tufts of straw, sands, fragments,
Buoyed hither from many moods, one contradicting
    another,
From the storm, the long calm, the darkness, the
    swell,
Musing, pondering, a breath, a briny tear, a dab of
    liquid or soil,

Up just as much out of fathomless workings
    fermented and thrown,
A limp blossom or two, torn, just as much over waves
    floating, drifted at random,
Just as much for us that sobbing dirge of Nature,
Just as much, whence we come, that blare of the
    cloud-trumpets;
We, capricious, brought hither, we know not whence,
    spread out before You, up there, walking or sitting,
Whoever you are – we too lie in drifts at your feet.

Out of the Cradle Endlessly Rocking

Out of the rocked cradle,
Out of the mocking-bird's throat, the musical shuttle,
Out of the boy's mother's womb, and from the
  nipples of her breasts,
Out of the Ninth Month midnight,
Over the sterile sands, and the fields beyond, where
  the child, leaving his bed, wandered alone,
  bareheaded, barefoot,
Down from the showered halo,
Up from the mystic play of shadows, twining and
  twisting as if they were alive,
Out from the patches of briers and blackberries,
From the memories of the bird that chanted to me,
From your memories, sad brother – from the fitful
  risings and fallings I heard,
From under that yellow half-moon, late-risen, and
  swollen as if with tears,
From those beginning notes of sickness and love,
  there in the transparent mist,
From the thousand responses of my heart, never to
  cease,
From the myriad thence-aroused words,
From the word stronger and more delicious than any,
From such, as now they start, the scene revisiting,

____

Original title: "A Word Out of the Sea"

As a flock, twittering, rising, or overhead passing,
Borne hither – ere all eludes me, hurriedly,
A man – yet by these tears a little boy again,
Throwing myself on the sand, confronting the waves,
I, chanter of pains and joys, uniter of here and
    hereafter,
Taking all hints to use them – but swiftly leaping
    beyond them,
A reminiscence sing.

REMINISCENCE

Once, Paumanok,
When the snows had melted, and the Fifth Month
    grass was growing,
Up this sea-shore, in some briers,
Two guests from Alabama – two together,
And their nest, and four light-green eggs, spotted
    with brown,
And every day the he-bird, to and fro, near at hand,
And every day the she-bird, crouched on her nest,
    silent, with bright eyes,
And every day I, a curious boy, never too close, never
    disturbing them,
Cautiously peering, absorbing, translating.

Shine! Shine!
Pour down your warmth, great Sun!

While we bask – we two together.

Two together!
Winds blow South, or winds blow North,
Day come white, or night come black,
Home, or rivers and mountains from home,
Singing all time, minding no time,
If we two but keep together.

Till of a sudden,
May-be killed, unknown to her mate,
One forenoon the she-bird crouched not on the nest,
Nor returned that afternoon, nor the next,
Nor ever appeared again.

And thenceforward, all summer, in the sound of the
    sea,
And at night, under the full of the moon, in calmer
    weather,
Over the hoarse surging of the sea,
Or flitting from brier to brier by day,
I saw, I heard at intervals, the remaining one, the
    he-bird,
The solitary guest from Alabama.

Blow! Blow!
Blow up sea-winds along Paumanok's shore;
I wait and I wait, till you blow my mate to me.

Yes, when the stars glistened,
All night long, on the prong of a moss-scallop'd stake,
Down, almost amid the slapping waves,
Sat the lone singer, wonderful, causing tears.

He called on his mate,
He poured forth the meanings which I, of all men,
    know.

Yes, my brother, I know,
The rest might not – but I have treasured every note,
For once, and more than once, dimly, down to the
    beach gliding,
Silent, avoiding the moonbeams, blending myself
    with the shadows,
Recalling now the obscure shapes, the echoes, the
    sounds and sights after their sorts,
The white arms out in the breakers tirelessly tossing,
I, with bare feet, a child, the wind wafting my hair,
Listened long and long.

Listened, to keep, to sing – now translating the notes,
Following you, my brother.

Soothe! Soothe!
Close on its wave soothes the wave behind,

And again another behind, embracing and lapping, every
    one close,
But my love soothes not me.

Low hangs the moon — it rose late,
O it is lagging — O I think it is heavy with love.

O madly the sea pushes upon the land,
With love — with love.

O night!
O do I not see my love fluttering out there among the
    breakers?
What is that little black thing I see there in the white?

Loud! Loud!
Loud I call to you my love!
High and clear I shoot my voice over the waves,
Surely you must know who is here,
You must know who I am, my love.

Low-hanging moon!
What is that dusky spot in your brown yellow?
O it is the shape of my mate!
O moon, do not keep her from me any longer.

Land! O land!
Whichever way I turn, O I think you could give me my
    mate back again, if you would,

For I am almost sure I see her dimly whichever way I
  look.

O rising stars!
Perhaps the one I want so much will rise with some of
  you.

O throat!
Sound clearer through the atmosphere!
Pierce the woods, the earth,
Somewhere listening to catch you must be the one I want.

Shake out, carols!
Solitary here – the night's carols!
Carols of lonesome love! Death's carols!
Carols under that lagging, yellow, waning moon!
O, under that moon, where she droops almost down into
  the sea!
O reckless, despairing carols.

But soft!
Sink low – soft!
Soft! Let me just murmur,
And do you wait a moment, you husky-noised sea,
For somewhere I believe I heard my mate responding to
  me,
So faint – I must be still to listen,
But not altogether still, for then she might not come
  immediately to me.

Hither, my love!
Here I am! Here!
With this just-sustained note I announce myself to you,
This gentle call is for you, my love.

Do not be decoyed elsewhere!
That is the whistle of the wind — it is not my voice,
That is the fluttering of the spray,
Those are the shadows of leaves.

O darkness! O in vain!
O I am very sick and sorrowful.

O brown halo in the sky, near the moon, drooping upon
*   the sea!*
O troubled reflection in the sea!
O throat! O throbbing heart!
O all — and I singing uselessly all the night.

Murmur! Murmur on!
O murmurs — you yourselves make me continue to sing, I
*   know not why.*

O past! O joy!
In the air — in the woods — over fields,
Loved! Loved! Loved! Loved! Loved!
Loved — but no more with me,
We two together no more.

The aria sinking,
All else continuing – the stars shining,
The winds blowing – the notes of the wondrous bird
    echoing,
With angry moans the fierce old mother yet, as ever,
    incessantly moaning,
On the sands of Paumanok's shore gray and rustling,
The yellow half-moon, enlarged, sagging down,
    drooping, the face of the sea almost touching,
The boy extatic – with his bare feet the waves, with
    his hair the atmosphere dallying,
The love in the heart pent, now loose, now at last
    tumultuously bursting,
The aria's meaning, the ears, the Soul, swiftly
    depositing,
The strange tears down the cheeks coursing,
The colloquy there – the trio – each uttering,
The undertone – the savage old mother, incessantly
    crying,
To the boy's Soul's questions sullenly timing – some
    drowned secret hissing,
To the outsetting bard of love.

Bird! (then said the boy's Soul,)
Is it indeed toward your mate you sing? or is it mostly
    to me?

For I that was a child, my tongue's use sleeping,
Now that I have heard you,
Now in a moment I know what I am for – I awake,
And already a thousand singers – a thousand songs,
    clearer, louder, more sorrowful than yours,
A thousand warbling echoes have started to life
    within me,
Never to die.

O throes!
O you demon, singing by yourself – projecting me,
O solitary me, listening – never more shall I cease
    imitating, perpetuating you,
Never more shall I escape,
Never more shall the reverberations,
Never more the cries of unsatisfied love be absent
    from me,
Never again leave me to be the peaceful child I was
    before what there, in the night,
By the sea, under the yellow and sagging moon,
The dusky demon aroused – the fire, the sweet hell
    within,
The unknown want, the destiny of me.

O give me some clew!
O if I am to have so much, let me have more!
O a word! O what is my destination?

O I fear it is henceforth chaos!
O how joys, dreads, convolutions, human shapes, and
    all shapes, spring as from graves around me!
O phantoms! you cover all the land, and all the sea!
O I cannot see in the dimness whether you smile or
    frown upon me;
O vapor, a look, a word! O well-beloved!
O you dear women's and men's phantoms!

A word then, (for I will conquer it,)
The word final, superior to all,
Subtle, sent up – what is it? – I listen;
Are you whispering it, and have been all the time,
    you sea-waves?
Is that it from your liquid rims and wet sands?

Answering, the sea,
Delaying not, hurrying not,
Whispered me through the night, and very plainly
    before daybreak,
Lisped to me constantly the low and delicious word
    DEATH,
And again Death – ever Death, Death, Death,
Hissing melodious, neither like the bird, nor like my
    aroused child's heart,
But edging near, as privately for me, rustling at my
    feet,

And creeping thence steadily up to my ears,
Death, Death, Death, Death, Death.

Which I do not forget,
But fuse the song of two together,
That was sung to me in the moonlight on Paumanok's
    gray beach,
With the thousand responsive songs, at random,
My own songs, awaked from that hour,
And with them the key, the word up from the waves,
The word of the sweetest song, and all songs,
That strong and delicious word which, creeping to
    my feet,
The sea whispered me.

When Lilacs Last in the Dooryard Bloom'd

1

When lilacs last in the door-yard bloom'd,
And the great star early droop'd in the western sky in
   the night,
I mourn'd … and yet shall mourn with
   ever-returning spring.

O ever-returning spring! trinity sure to me you bring;
Lilac blooming perennial, and drooping star in the
   west,
And thought of him I love.

2

O powerful, western, fallen star!
O shades of night! O moody, tearful night!
O great star disappear'd! O the blank murk that hides
   the star!
O cruel hands that hold me powerless! O helpless soul
   of me!
O harsh surrounding cloud that will not free my soul!

3

In the door-yard fronting an old farm-house, near the
   white-wash'd palings,

Stands the lilac bush, tall-growing, with heart-shaped
    leaves of rich green,
With many a pointed blossom, rising, delicate, with
    the perfume strong I love,
With every leaf a miracle......and from this bush in
    the door-yard,
With its delicate-color'd blossoms, and heart-shaped
    leaves of rich green,
A sprig, with its flower, I break.

4

In the swamp, in secluded recesses,
A shy and hidden bird is warbling a song.

Solitary, the thrush,
The hermit, withdrawn to himself, avoiding the
    settlements,
Sings by himself a song.

Song of the bleeding throat!
Death's outlet song of life – (for well, dear brother, I
    know,
If thou wast not gifted to sing, thou would'st surely
    die.)

5

Over the breast of the spring, the land, amid cities,
Amid lanes, and through old woods, (where lately the
    violets peep'd from the ground, spotting the gray
    debris;)
Amid the grass in the fields each side of the lanes –
    passing the endless grass;
Passing the yellow-spear'd wheat, every grain from
    its shroud in the dark-brown fields uprising;
Passing the apple-tree blows of white and pink in the
    orchards;
Carrying a corpse to where it shall rest in the grave,
Night and day journeys a coffin.

6

Coffin that passes through lanes and streets,
Through day and night, with the great cloud
    darkening the land,
With the pomp of the inloop'd flags, with the cities
    draped in black,
With the show of the States themselves, as of
    crape-veil'd women, standing,
With processions long and winding, and the
    flambeaus of the night,
With the countless torches lit – with the silent sea of
    faces, and the unbared heads,

With the waiting depot, the arriving coffin, and the
    somber faces,
With dirges through the night, with the thousand
    voices rising strong and solemn;
With all the mournful voices of the dirges, pour'd
    around the coffin,
The dim-lit churches and the shuddering organs –
    Where amid these you journey,
With the tolling, tolling bells' perpetual clang;
Here! coffin that slowly passes.
I give you my sprig of lilac.

7

(Nor for you, for one, alone;
Blossoms and branches green to coffins all I bring:
For fresh as the morning – thus would I chant a song
    for you, O sane and sacred death.

All over bouquets of roses,
O death! I cover you over with roses and early lilies;
But mostly and now the lilac that blooms the first,
Copious, I break, I break the sprigs from the bushes:
With loaded arms I come, pouring for you,
For you and the coffins all of you, O death.)

8

O western orb, sailing the heaven!

Now I know what you must have meant, as a month
  since we walk'd,
As we walk'd up and down in the dark blue so
  mystic,
As we walk'd in silence the transparent shadowy
  night,
As I saw you had something to tell, as you bent to me
  night after night,
As you droop'd from the sky low down, as if to my
  side, (while the other stars all look'd on;)
As we wander'd together the solemn night, (for
  something I know not what, kept me from sleep;)
As the night advanced, and I saw on the rim of the
  west, ere you went, how full you were of woe;
As I stood on the rising ground in the breeze, in the
  cool transparent night,
As I watch'd where you pass'd and was lost in the
  netherward black of the night,
As my soul, in its trouble, dissatisfied, sank, as where
  you, sad orb,
Concluded, dropt in the night, and was gone.

9

Sing on, there in the swamp!
O singer bashful and tender! I hear your notes – I
  hear your call;
I hear – I come presently – I understand you;

But a moment I linger – for the lustrous star has
    detain'd me;
The star, my comrade, departing, holds and detains
    me.

10

O how shall I warble myself for the dead one there I
    loved?
And how shall I deck my song for the large sweet soul
    that has gone?
And what shall my perfume be, for the grave of him I
    love?

Sea-winds, blown from east and west,
Blown from the eastern sea, and blown from the
    western sea, till there on the prairies meeting:
These, and with these, and the breath of my chant,
I perfume the grave of him I love.

11

O what shall I hang on the chamber walls?
And what shall the pictures be that I hang on the
    walls,
To adorn the burial-house of him I love?
Pictures of growing spring, and farms, and homes,
With the Fourth-month eve at sundown, and the
    gray-smoke lucid and bright,

With floods of the yellow gold of the gorgeous,
    indolent, sinking sun, burning, expanding the air;
With the fresh sweet herbage under foot, and the pale
    green leaves of the trees prolific;
In the distance the flowing glaze, the breast of the
    river, with a wind-dapple here and there;
With ranging hills on the banks, with many a line
    against the sky, and shadows;
And the city at hand, with dwellings so dense, and
    stacks of chimneys,
And all the scenes of life, and the workshops, and the
    workmen homeward returning.

12

Lo! body and soul! this land!
Mighty Manhattan, with spires, and the sparkling and
    hurrying tides, and the ships;
The varied and ample land – the South and the North
    in the light – Ohio's shores, and flashing Missouri,
And ever the far-spreading prairies, cover'd with
    grass and corn.

Lo! the most excellent sun, so calm and haughty;
The violet and purple morn, with just-felt breezes:
The gentle, soft-born, measureless light;
The miracle, spreading, bathing all – the fulfill'd
    noon;

The coming eve, delicious – the welcome night, and
    the stars,
Over my cities shining all, enveloping man and land.

13

Sing on! sing on, you gray-brown bird!
Sing from the swamps, the recesses – pour your chant
    from the bushes;
Limitless out of the dusk, out of the cedars and pines.
Sing on, dearest brother – warble your reedy song;
Loud human song, with voice of uttermost woe.

O liquid, and free, and tender!
O wild and loose to my soul! O wondrous singer!
You only I hear......yet the star holds me, (but will
    soon depart;)
Yet the lilac, with mastering odor, holds me.

14

Now while I sat in the day, and look'd forth,
In the close of the day, with its light, and the fields of
    spring, and the farmer preparing his crops,
In the large unconscious scenery of my land, with its
    lakes and forests,
In the heavenly aerial beauty, (after the perturb'd
    winds, and the storms;)

194

Under the arching heavens of the afternoon swift
    passing, and the voices of children and women,
The many-moving sea-tides, – and I saw the ships
    how they sail'd,
And the summer approaching with richness, and the
    fields all busy with labor,
And the infinite separate houses, how they all went
    on, each with its meals and minutia of daily usages;
And the streets, how their throbbings throbb'd, and
    the cities pent, – lo! then and there,
Falling among them all, and upon them all,
    enveloping me with the rest,
Appear'd the cloud, appear'd the long black trail;
And I knew Death, its thought, and the sacred
    knowledge of death.

15

Then with the knowledge of death as walking one
    side of me,
And the thought of death close-walking the other side
    of me,
And I in the middle, as with companions, and as
    holding the hands of companions,
I fled forth to the hiding receiving night, that talks
    not,
Down to the shores of the water, the path by the
    swamp in the dimness,

To the solemn shadowy cedars, and ghostly pines so
     still.

And the singer so shy to the rest receiv'd me;
The gray-brown bird I know, receiv'd us comrades
     three;
And he sang what seem'd the song of death, and a
     verse for him I love.

From deep secluded recesses,
From the fragrant cedars, and the ghostly pines so
     still,
Came the singing of the bird.

And the charm of the singing rapt me,
As I held, as if by their hands, my comrades in the
     night;
And the voice of my spirit tallied the song of the bird.

16

Come, lovely and soothing Death,
Undulate round the world, serenely arriving,
     arriving,
In the day, in the night, to all, to each,
Sooner or later, delicate Death.

Prais'd be the fathomless universe,

For life and joy, and for objects and knowledge
    curious;
And for love, sweet love – But praise! O praise and
    praise,
For the sure-enwinding arms of cool-enfolding
    Death.

Dark Mother, always gliding near, with soft feet,
Have none chanted for thee a chant of fullest
    welcome?
Then I chant it for thee – I glorify thee above all;
I bring thee a song that when thou must indeed come,
    come unfalteringly.

Approach, encompassing Death – strong Deliveress!
When it is so – when thou hast taken them, I joyously
    sing the dead,
Lost in the loving, floating ocean of thee,
Laved in the flood of thy bliss, O Death.

From me to thee glad serenades,
Dances for thee I propose, saluting thee – adornments
    and feastings for thee;
And the sights of the open landscape, and the
    high-spread sky, are fitting,
And life and the fields, and the huge and thoughtful
    night.

The night, in silence, under many a star;
The ocean shore, and the husky whispering wave,
    whose voice I know;
And the soul turning to thee, O vast and well-veil'd
    Death,
And the body gratefully nestling close to thee.

Over the tree-tops I float thee a song!
Over the rising and sinking waves – over the myriad
    fields, and the prairies wide;
Over the dense-pack'd cities all, and the teeming
    wharves and ways,
I float this carol with joy, with joy to thee, O Death!

17

To the tally of my soul,
Loud and strong kept up the gray-brown bird,
With pure, deliberate notes, spreading, filling the
    night.

Loud in the pines and cedars dim,
Clear in the freshness moist, and the swamp-perfume;
And I with my comrades there in the night.

While my sight that was bound in my eyes unclosed,
As to long panoramas of visions.

18

I saw the vision of armies;
And I saw, as in noiseless dreams, hundreds of
  battle-flags;
Borne through the smoke of the battles, and pierc'd
  with missiles, I saw them,
And carried hither and yon through the smoke, and
  torn and bloody;
And at last but a few shreds of the flags left on the
  staffs, (and all in silence,)
And the staffs all splinter'd and broken.

I saw battle-corpses, myriads of them,
And the white skeletons of young men – I saw them;
I saw the debris and debris of all dead soldiers;
But I saw they were not as was thought;
They themselves were fully at rest – they suffer'd
  not;
The living remain'd and suffer'd – the mother
  suffer'd,
And the wife and the child, and the musing comrade
  suffer'd,
And the armies that remain'd suffer'd.

19

Passing the visions, passing the night;
Passing, unloosing the hold of my comrades' hands;
Passing the song of the hermit bird, and the tallying
  song of my soul,
Victorious song, death's outlet song, (yet varying,
  ever-altering song,
As low and wailing, yet clear the notes, rising and
  falling, flooding the night,
Sadly sinking and fainting, as warning and warning,
  and yet again bursting with joy,)
Covering the earth, and filling the spread of the
  heaven,
As that powerful psalm in the night I heard from
  recesses.

20

Must I leave thee, lilac with heart-shaped leaves?
Must I leave thee there in the door-yard, blooming,
  returning with spring?
Must I pass from my song for thee;
From my gaze on thee in the west, fronting the west,
  communing with thee,
O comrade lustrous, with silver face in the night?

Yet each I keep, and all;
The song, the wondrous chant of the gray-brown
  bird, I keep,
And the tallying chant, the echo arous'd in my soul, I
  keep,
With the lustrous and drooping star, with the
  countenance full of woe;
With the lilac tall, and its blossoms of mastering odor;
Comrades mine, and I in the midst, and their memory
  ever I keep – for the dead I loved so well;
For the sweetest, wisest soul of all my days and lands
  … and this for his dear sake;
Lilac and star and bird, twined with the chant of my
  soul,
With the holders holding my hand, nearing the call of
  the bird,
There in the fragrant pines, and the cedars dusk and
  dim.